FEB - - 2021

IN PRAISE OF PATHS

TRANSLATION BY
BECKY L. CROOK

TORBJØRN EKELUND

FOREWORD BY
GEOFF NICHOLSON

IN PRAISE OF PATHS

WALKING THROUGH TIME AND NATURE

GREYSTONE BOOKS
Vancouver/Berkeley

Greystone Books Ltd.
greystonebooks.com

Cataloguing data available from Library and Archives Canada
ISBN 978-1-77164-495-2 (cloth)
ISBN 978-1-77164-496-9 (epub)

Copy editing by Lucy Kenward
Proofreading by Stefania Alexandru
Jacket and text design by Belle Wuthrich
Typesetting by Fiona Siu
Printed and bound in Canada on ancient-forest-friendly paper by Friesens

Greystone Books gratefully acknowledges the Musqueam, Squamish, and Tsleil-Waututh peoples on whose land our office is located.

Greystone Books thanks the Canada Council for the Arts, the British Columbia Arts Council, the Province of British Columbia through the Book Publishing Tax Credit, and the Government of Canada for supporting our publishing activities.

This translation has been published with the financial support of NORLA.

Canadä

CONTENTS

*The world reveals itself
to those who travel on foot.*
WERNER HERZOG

FOREWORD

ONE EXTRAORDINARY SIDE effect of reading Torbjørn Ekelund's *In Praise of Paths* is that as I wander through the world I now constantly ask myself, "Is this really a path that I'm walking on?" Sometimes the answer's an unequivocal yes, and on some occasions I know I'm walking on a special *kind* of path: a footpath, a garden path, a tow path, a bridle path. This is all very reassuring.

But at other times the question gets far more complicated. I ask myself, "Am I perhaps walking on a trail or a track, along a lane or a pedestrian way or a desire line?" In the part of England that I come from there are also gennels (sometimes jinnels), and elsewhere in England there are snickets and twittens. I find myself wondering whether these are types of path, or whether they're physically and philosophically something quite different, perhaps not paths at all.

Well, I don't have any hard-and-fast answers to these questions, and fortunately, Torbjørn Ekelund doesn't seem to either—he is not a dogmatic writer or thinker, which is just as well. And perhaps my occasional puzzlement may be an indication that a path is not such a simple thing as it first appears, as many would suppose, which is to say that a path is rarely "just" a path. Yes, it may be a means of getting from A to B (or Z), but it can very often be metaphorical or allegorical as well.

Ekelund points out that if you google the word "path" you'll "have to scroll through countless religious or spiritual references, pages about yoga, meditation, mindfulness, everything other than a physical path." There will also be references to Buddhism, Hinduism, Christianity, and Islam, all of which, one way or another, employ the idea of the path as a symbol of spiritual progress and development.

In your online search you might well also find some much less spiritual usages, such as the Shining Path— Peru's revolutionary communist group founded in the late 1960s, or Annie Besant's *My Path to Atheism*, written in 1878. All roads lead to the path, it seems.

You may also find admonitions to stick to the straight and narrow path, but no serious traveler or walker would obey that rule, and Ekelund certainly doesn't. He roams, he strays, he meanders, he wanders off the beaten path, both physically and intellectually, in all the best possible ways.

His range of references is especially interesting and novel to an Anglophone reader. Sometimes the pathfinders he refers to are the well-known usual suspects—Virginia Woolf, Emma Gatewood, Edward Payson Weston, Werner Herzog, but he introduces us to a lot of far less familiar—generally Scandinavian—figures, such as Bjørn Amsrud, the first person to walk the length of Norway; and the philosopher Arne Næss, who regularly hiked to his mountaintop cabin but always went by a different route. I was especially fascinated by Joshua French, a Norwegian mercenary jailed in the Democratic Republic of the Congo, who spent every day of his incarceration walking back and forth along a corridor that was only fifty feet long. I was also pleased to discover the Norwegian word *friluftsliv,* a word in one sense meaning simply "fresh air life" but carrying with it the philosophy that spending time outdoors is essential to physical and mental health. These ideas in themselves might send a reader to do some more googling, or perhaps even to take a trip to a well-stocked library.

One of the things Ekelund gets absolutely right is the delicate balance between the general and the specific, between the public and the private, between the grand narrative and a wholly personal one. He shows that paths take us forward but they also take us back into the past and into our selves. He describes the many walks he's taken as an adult, but these lead him back to a path that went to the cabin where he spent childhood vacations with his family. He revisits the place both on foot and in his memory, to create some wonderfully moving passages about the flow of time, and about mortality.

In the Zen sense, we obviously can't walk the same path twice; both the path and our selves are different at every moment. But Ekelund also tells us, if we need to be told—and perhaps we do—that the path we walk today always connects with paths that others have taken before us, and that paths always involve a connection with other walkers. He writes, "No single person is responsible for a path; instead, it is the sum of the actions of numerous people over a time that dates back to the distant past." This strikes me as a very profound perception; something that we recognize as obviously true the moment we think about it, and yet most of us have never thought about it in quite that way.

There are two other pieces of Ekelund wisdom that I know will live with me. First, that "The history of the path is the history of us," and second, that "The path is order in chaos." Words to live by, and words by which to lose and find yourself.

—GEOFF NICHOLSON

ON MISTAKEN POINT, at the mouth of the fjord on the southeastern point of Newfoundland, Canada, is a track, a footprint. It measures a half an inch wide, seven inches long, and is 565 million years old. The track stretches across a gray rock with a crack down the center. It is not a straight line; rather, the movement indicates small, sideways motions and uneven edges. There is a clear starting point to the track, as if the creature that made it had been lying dormant for quite some time before finally beginning to stir. At the opposite end, the track has been wiped away before becoming less visible until, in the end, it vanishes completely. By all appearances, the track was made by a slow-moving creature, a snail or something not unlike a snail.

The discovery of this fossil track in the 1960s caused a small sensation, because the life-form that made it apparently had the ability to propel itself by its own will from one location to another. It is both as simple and as complex as that. The track on Mistaken Point is the first documented evidence of voluntary movement in the history of the earth. Voluntary movement is the prerequisite for paths.

THE BEGINNING

W E WERE NOMADS once. We migrated, never remaining for long in a single location. The world lay open and undiscovered, borderless. We could walk in any direction, follow our will, explore new lands.

Now we are sedentary. We live our lives sitting down. Drive the car to the store. Fly if traveling longer distances. Call to have the pizza delivered to our door and purchase automatic lawn mowers, robots to do the work for us while we sit sunning and thinking about more pressing matters than mowing the lawn.

The journey has lost its original purpose. It is no longer an essential undertaking to sustain our lives; rather, it has become a form of amusement and recreation. We board an airplane in one corner of the world and disembark in another. We have the ability to put enormous distances behind us without expending any of our own energy or gaining any knowledge about the paths and landscapes that lie unfurled beneath the cloud cover several thousand feet below. A lot has changed and a lot has been lost when checking in at the airport is the most energy-intensive stage of a journey that relocates us from one side of the globe to the other.

Our ability to read a landscape used to be indispensable for survival. Now we no longer require any knowledge of navigation and orienteering to get where we want to go. The path is displayed on our smartphones, our GPS, and as we walk we stare down at a lit screen instead of up at the place where we are and the path we are on. Our sense of place has become an aptitude we would prefer to do without. The same is true for our sense of distance.

PATHS WERE THE first main thoroughfares, and the way in which they meander and wind through the landscape tells us something very fundamental about the people who created them. A path's line is never accidental. It is not the shortest distance between two points; it is the simplest. It is a result of the intrinsic human inclination to choose the path of least resistance, because conserving energy used to be so critical for survival.

Messengers traveled by foot on paths or carriage roads. The time it took to walk the path was secondary to the energy it required. Upon arrival, the message may already have become outdated and possibly even untrue. "Everyone is doing fine," the letter may have said, read by a European immigrant to America from relatives back home, though in the months that had passed since the letter was posted, many of those relatives, perhaps even the letter-writer, may have died of hunger, tuberculosis, scarlet fever, or in childbirth.

The premise for all travel was that it took time. The war might well be over by the time the messenger arrived to say it had just broken out.

THE HISTORY OF paths is also the history of a world on the verge of disappearing. First, paths transformed into roads, feet became wagons and horse carriages, dirt was replaced with asphalt and concrete. More recently, wagons and horse carriages have been switched out for cars and heavy transport vehicles, roads have been widened, swamps drained, mountains blown up, and plains leveled with a layer of crushed gravel.

The duration of a journey used to be determined by the path. Today it is possible to adapt and reconfigure the landscape. Mountains can be blasted, wetlands drained, rivers diverted into pipes. We have all but eliminated the barriers of physical space in travel. Time, however, has now become the most important factor.

In the anecdote "The Road," Norwegian author and philosopher Peter Wessel Zapffe writes:

> *This is how the path came to the world, through the foot's meeting with soft humus, and the people and the path grew up together, and shared both good and bad days.... One day something new happened. A loud, stinking vehicle for trolls jolted and smashed its way up through the valley.... Then came the engineers. Strange men with iron skeletons and angular brains and eyes of quartz for seeing beams. They screeched and hacked and with thunder and smoke dragged a bleeding stone artery as wide as a barn behind them through the mountain.... The new road charged ahead like a madman, deaf and blind to everything except the goal.*

Paths once blended into the landscape; they did not destroy it. But roads did. The advent of roads changed everything. They not only reshaped the original landscape, they also became a hindrance for the migration that is instinctive to the brown bear, the reindeer, the salmon, the wolf, almost all living creatures, seasonal migrants—migrations for food, their endless trek from one place to another and back again.

The migration routes of animals were interrupted by large unpassable roadways. The seasonal routes of birds were sundered by flying metal monstrosities that suddenly dominated the airspace. The annual fish runs were cut off by dams and bridges that blocked the rivers. Species lost their habitats and died out.

✦

WHEN I WAS a child, paths were a common thread that ran consistently throughout my life. Walking was a natural part of being; there was no way around it. Paths were everywhere.

Then I grew up and began working in an office. The paths disappeared out of my life, as did movement. Signs pointed out where I should go. Asphalt ensured all my steps were even. Street lamps drove away the dark. Gates and curbs guided me in the right direction.

I no longer discovered things. I no longer had to look around at my surroundings to figure out where I was and where to go. I no longer needed to trust my own judgement and decide on the best direction. A life of movement had shifted to a static one. I drove a car to get somewhere, and if I wanted to go somewhere but did not have access to a car, I often decided I might as well stay home.

ONE DAY SOMETHING happened that would change my life for the worse, as well as for the better. I interviewed an author. We sat across from each other at a large white table in an office in downtown Oslo. The author was telling me about a book he had written. I tried to listen but suddenly it felt like my head was no longer working, as if everything had shut down inside. I stared at the author. I could see his mouth moving but I could no longer comprehend what he was saying. The last thing I remember thinking was: What is going to happen to me now?

When I woke up, I was in an ambulance. A man was talking to me. His face hovered overhead, large and blurry. I noticed he was wearing a red jacket with yellow reflective stripes. "Can you hear me," the man said, "can you hear me?" I tried to respond but found I could not. It felt as if I were lying on the bottom of the ocean. I wanted to swim up to the man with the red jacket but he was so far away and I didn't have the strength. I opened my mouth to say something. Then everything went black again.

A few hours later, I awoke in the hospital. I was in a bed that people were rolling around from place to place. Nurses and doctors came and went. They told me things I didn't understand and spoke in a language I didn't know. They examined my head: MRI, CAT scans.

Took X-rays of my entire body. They didn't find anything. Everything appeared normal, and yet something dramatic had happened.

I was put up in one of the hospital rooms and slowly transformed back into myself. My language abilities returned; my memory came back. I stayed in that room for three days until a doctor came in and informed me that I had developed epilepsy. "A number of things in your life are going to change now," said the doctor, "and one of them is that you will no longer be permitted to drive a car."

On my last day in hospital, I lay thinking about this change. My driver's license of almost thirty years had been revoked. The first thing I thought was that this was going to have big practical consequences. I have heard that people with illnesses leading to the loss of their driver's license experience the fact they can no longer drive a car as a heavier blow than the illness itself. How would it affect me? Was my life going to change completely? Would I miss our old Volvo?

AFTER I WAS released from the hospital, I hung up my car keys once and for all. However, what happened next amazed me, and it amazes me still. I had been issued an entirely new identity, but it only took me a matter of days to get used to it. I was no longer someone who drove a car. Instead, I was someone who got around on foot. The adjustment was not nearly as frustrating as I had imagined it would be. In fact, it was liberating. I changed my habits and I didn't seem to miss a thing. My pace of life slowed, my pulse decreased, and the world opened up to me in a way I had not experienced since I was a child.

I walked to all the places I needed to go, and this is how the paths came back into my life. If the path was wide and dry, the going was quick. If it was steep and wet, I walked more slowly. The time it took became meaningless. Space once again became the primary factor of travel.

This was both a revelation and a relief. Suddenly I could see paths everywhere, thoroughfares I'd never known existed. Narrow paths cutting across green lawns; animal paths through the woods; shortcuts through hedges, in and out of gardens, across fields and parking lots. I even became aware of my own ingrained patterns of movement throughout my house.

I began to try out new ways of walking. I would walk quickly and I would walk slowly. I would walk with a heavy or an empty backpack; wearing big boots or wearing light running shoes.

During my summer vacations I walked barefoot. For the entire month of July I hardly wore anything on my feet. When autumn arrived, I walked to work with my eyes shut. It was a peculiar whim and the people I encountered must have thought I was insane, but I wasn't. I merely wanted to see how it felt. Without vision to guide me, my attention was entirely focused on the movement of the body. I felt how my feet were working. The shift of weight from one leg to the other. How one foot landed on the heel, rolled forward over the balls of my feet, how the toes pushed off at the same moment when the other foot landed on its heel, in perfect coordination. My arms created momentum, swinging in balance with my legs: the left arm forward, the right leg behind, in a complex interplay that held my body in balance while propelling me forward at the same time. I felt how my thigh and leg muscles pushed my body ahead, and how small muscles I didn't know existed were supporting my body and helping recover my balance as required. The human foot is composed of twenty-six bones working together in an intricately choreographed sequence. I had never given them a spare thought, but now I felt able to appreciate the movement of each and every one. My spine was erect, my head held up, and my face turned forward, even if my eyes were closed.

I walked to work like a sleepwalker. I noticed sounds I'd never heard before. Airplanes taking off and landing at the airport. Car engines revving up and turning off. I heard the tick from the pedestrian-crossing signal at the traffic lights. The nuance in birdsong, the distant whine of ambulance sirens. The bus pulling up to a stop and heaving a sigh as its doors clapped open. I heard dry autumn leaves rustling in the morning wind. Children on their way to school, high-pitched conversations, shuffling steps. Someone sweeping the stairs in front of their house. A letter carrier sticking the post into mailboxes: first lifting the flap of the boxes and then shoving the papers inside, as if filled with a violent rage that needed to be expelled. I heard the rush of the city—sounds that were hard to distinguish except as the din of a thousand different tasks, none of which had to do with ambling on a sidewalk with one's eyes closed.

I WALKED AND walked, and for every yard I put behind me, I felt the urge to walk farther. I read about famous long-distance hiking trails. The John Muir Trail in the US. The Laugavegur Trail in Iceland. The King's Trail in Sweden. The Great Divide Trail in Canada. The South West Coast Path in England. The Goldsteig Trail in Germany. Te Araroa in New Zealand.

In the evenings, I unfolded maps across the table and studied them under the kitchen's yellow light. The paths wound like rivers over the maps, up into the mountains, along the uneven banks of waterways, up ridges, around swamps, and across wide plateaus.

It was possible I would never walk these paths. They were very long. Epic distances intended for those of a tougher ilk than me. They required months to complete from start to finish. Their completion assumed you had good finances at your disposal and the possibility of time off from work. Or that you were young enough not to be responsible for anyone other than yourself.

Still, there were other ways to go about it, to cover long distances without traveling across the world or breaking the bank, because paths resemble each other. Paths are all guided by the same inherent logic, regardless of whether they are short or long, magnificent or hideous, or located in China or India, on the Russian taiga or in a forest close to Oslo. I had at my disposal narrow paths and paths that were old, overgrown and fresh, manicured, as well as paths I knew and some I had never explored. I could read books about paths, dive into whatever literature might exist on the topic. I wanted to learn more about how paths came to be and why, about nomadic peoples, about migration and movement, orienteering, navigation, and why we no longer walk.

I WALKED AND wrote, walked and wrote, and the more I walked and the more I wrote, the clearer it became to me that the history of the path cannot be told without also telling the history of walking humans and the landscapes that surrounded them. Paths and the landscape are inextricably bound. It's the same with humans. We understand ourselves in relation to the landscape of our birth. More than any other factor, the environment in which we are born establishes the reference points for our lives. When we move through a landscape, we are doing something that feels innate. We are moving in the way we were meant to move. Our tempo enables us to look around and take the world in, to observe the shift that comes with slowing down, to hear sounds; recognize smells; feel the wind, sun, and rain in our face; and contemplate the purpose of the outing, which may shift as we walk.

Paths are the story of humans journeying on foot. They have a beginning, a middle, and an end. They point forward toward the journey's goal but also behind to all who have traveled this same path before us, including those who created the first track. The history of paths is the history of us: countless stories about labor and sustenance, exploration and migration, a web spun around the earth like thread from a ball of yarn.

This book tells some of those stories.

THE MEASURE OF
ALL PATHS

W HEN I WAS a child, my family owned a small
wooden cabin. The cabin was next to a lake
north of the little coastal city of Larvik, about
two hours south of Norway's capital city, Oslo. The
closest village was called Lysebo, a name implying light,
so we called the cabin Solli, which implies sunlight on
a hillside. The cabin sat off on its own at the edge of the
forest, with enough elevation to have a view out over
the large lake. It was here that our family of five—my
mother, my father, my two sisters, and I—spent all of our
free time, weekends and holidays, year after year. It was
the hub that bound us together and made us a family.

Behind the cabin was a path. It wasn't long; it didn't
pass through magnificent landscapes or boast grand

vistas or points of interest along the way. It wasn't even marked on a map. But it was the first path I ever walked, and I remember it well because once, long ago, it was the only path I knew.

The path crossed a field and entered the forest. It led past a mountain, across a bridge, along a stream. I had no idea who first created the path, or why. It simply existed, a natural component of my childhood's primary landscape. Whenever we visited the cabin, we would walk on the path. My sisters and I walked ahead, and my mother and father walked behind. We walked to where the path ended and took a break. And then we turned around and retraced our steps back home.

When we returned to the cabin, we were released from all obligations for the remainder of the day. "You may play inside now," my mother would say, smiling. We had been nomadic for a brief period and were allowed to be civilized again. It was a principle we had been raised to follow: if you want to sit still, you first have to move around.

My mother had also walked on that path ever since her childhood. She would point and explain as we walked. "That's where we rode with the horse and wagon." "That mountain is where the horse rested." "This is where strawberries grow in the summer; that's where mushrooms come up in the fall." "This is where the cowslips grow; that's where we would go to get a Christmas tree; here is where the moose pass through; that is where the reindeer walk; this is Grandma's hepatica patch."

Each time we walked on the path, we got to know it better and after a few years we had it memorized. We knew the variations in elevation and the path's turns through the terrain. We knew where it felt easy to walk and at what point the energy in our tiny bodies began to abandon us.

We gave names to the various places we passed. The names highlighted only the most obvious characteristics of the landscape, nothing else. The Waterfall. The Mountain. The Field. The Creek. As if nothing other than a waterfall, a mountain, a field, a creek, and a single path existed in all the world. In those days, I didn't know the globe was crisscrossed with paths formed by every kind of living being, from the most miniscule to the most gigantic, and that paths have existed for as long as such beings have walked the earth.

Since that time, we have grown up and become adults, my sisters and I. We have started our own families, moved into cities, and found other places to spend our vacations. Nearly ten years have passed since I set foot on that little path, but I have walked it in my thoughts over and over again. Whenever life seems too stressful or filled with too many goals or hard decisions to make, as I lie in bed trying to fall asleep I shut my eyes and walk along the path, not unlike the way a downhill ski racer visualizes the course before pushing off and allowing gravity to take over. I note every detail in the landscape—the turns, the shifts in elevation—the way I did when I was younger, and every time I walk the path in my mind, it changes. I add or subtract something, which is what always happens when we recall our memories. That's how memories are formed, in the intersection between reality and fantasy, and this is precisely how it has been with my memories of the path.

✦

ONE DAY IN early spring, I visited my dad. I hadn't been to see him in a long time. He had been cleaning out the house and come across a few old photographs, he told me, and we sat down at the kitchen table to look at them. The photographs were over forty years old and they all depicted variations on the same theme: my sisters and me in different outdoor settings. We were on a walk through the forest, at the lake, on the mountain. My mother was rarely in any of the photographs and my father was never in them; he was the one who took the pictures.

Two of the photos caught my attention.

In the first, my sisters and I are sitting on the sofa in the little cabin. We are seated close together and we are staring at the camera. On the coffee table in front of us are three Easter eggs and the cage of the parakeet Jakob, the only pet I have ever owned.

In the second photograph, we are walking hand in hand down the little path. I sat at my father's kitchen table, staring at this photograph. Suddenly I could remember the landscape around the path. I could hear the sounds; sense the smells; feel the cold fresh air, the trickle of the rain, the rustle of my pants with every step I took. I could feel my rubber boots sinking into the soft grass each time I put a foot down.

The second photograph is taken from behind. It shows my sisters and me just before we've reached the cabin at the end of our hike. I am walking between them. All three of us are carrying tiny backpacks: mine is blue; my sisters both have red ones. We are wearing hats and holding hands. The photo was taken on a chilly day. The air is thick with rain. The trees stand leafless, barren. The grass is flat and gray. From the surrounding landscape, it looks to be late fall or early spring.

As I sat at my father's kitchen table staring at the old photo, I realized for the first time that every path in my life has been measured against that one small path behind our cabin. I understood that I had to return and walk that path again, to find out if it was still there or if it had been swallowed up by grass and moss, consumed by the surrounding landscape. Would it be as I remembered it? Or had these past four decades altered it so much that it now existed only in my memory?

PART
I

HUMANS
HAVE ALWAYS
WANDERED

THE FIRST THING humans did after they climbed down from the trees on the savannahs of Africa 200,000 years ago was walk. We belonged to a hunter-gatherer culture, which meant we were always on the move, following our prey, discovering new lands. Life consisted of movement; we did not yet have any concept of a sedentary lifestyle.

We wandered. And wherever we went, we left behind paths that were later followed by others. This is how paths were formed through the great, godless land. They are a visible result of the ceaseless migration of animals and humans across continents over centuries.

The world changed. Old paths were washed away, new ones were formed and, with them, new stories. Eleven thousand years ago, the last glacial period ended. The northern hemisphere had been covered by an enormous continental ice cap for over 100,000 years. The ice receded and the land rose up. Humans felt the irresistible urge to explore these new lands and to follow the edge of the ice northward to see what they would find there. They followed the game animals because they needed food. But they were also curious, as humans tend to be—driven not only by the need for sustenance but also by a powerful desire to investigate.

They were living toward the end of the Old Stone Age, in a culture that would last for many thousands of years before humans developed agriculture and domesticated animals.

FOR A LONG time now, we seem to have forgotten that migration is natural, a lifestyle that has long been part of human history. Though nomadic peoples make up only a tiny percentage of the population today, they still exist. The Sami in Norway. Some cultures in Africa. The Roma people in Europe who live as they have always done, moving from city to city and country to country, and who are still considered pariahs.

Emigration and immigration are not unnatural; rather, staying in one place is. And yet our culture can hardly tolerate the nomadic way of life. When we fill out official documents, the phrase "no fixed address" is often one of the options listed. But as anyone who fills out forms like these knows, there is no advantage to checking off this particular box. Those who are not settled can easily vanish. They cannot put down roots. They are not considered trustworthy.

The word "restless" signals someone who is unable to rest, to pause, to stop and settle down. This term carries negative connotations. Children who can't sit still on their chairs are given diagnoses. Children who sit still are praised. No one seems to consider anymore that perhaps it should be the other way around.

Streams of refugees spur fierce debates and deep rifts among permanent residents, and situations like these might continue to get worse. If humans are unable to reduce the temperatures on this planet, extreme weather patterns will inevitably lead to more drought, increased flooding, rising oceans, ruined crops, and greater displacement and migration. Millions of people might be forced to flee their current homes. Doing so will feel like the only natural course of action. They will abandon their homes and wander because this relocation is their sole chance for survival. In the not-too-distant future, our continents, states, and cities are going to experience larger exoduses and immigrations than at any point yet in human history.

HUMANS OF THE Stone Age were masters at orienting themselves in unfamiliar landscapes, reading the terrain, and finding their way forward. Their chosen path may not have been the shortest distance, nor the most expedient, but it was the path of least resistance. This trait characterized paths back then, and it continues to characterize them now. A route that follows the path of least resistance through uncharted territory is intuitively understood because it taps into an instinct that is deeply ingrained in all of us.

Paths formed because those who walked left behind footprints in the dirt as they traveled. Others who followed left new footprints on top of the old ones, ensuring the original tracks were not wiped out by natural phenomena before someone else passed the same way.

The path originated for itself. It was not a scenic route through landscape designed as a promenade or a showcase for breathtaking vistas. It was not planned. There were no preliminary reports, no feasibility studies, no prior thought given to grading or paving.

The path is an effect, not a cause. It is organic and biodegradable, conforms to the landscape, is a part of the very natural world it passes through. It is temporary; its use and its existence are interdependent. It is there because someone uses it and it is used because it is there. To maintain a path is to walk it.

Paths resemble legends, myths, folk ballads, fairy tales. They originated from a collective and cannot be traced back to one particular author. They have a body and a soul, at once material and immaterial. A path is more than a mere thoroughfare.

A path is the opposite of a straight line. Whereas a path is real, a straight line is a mental experiment, a theoretical construct. Straight lines don't exist in the concrete world: not even the surface of the water is straight, not even beams of light from the sun.

A path is the least possible encroachment upon nature. It belongs there, as a natural part of the terrain.

A path is always small, which is why it is called a path. If it expands and becomes larger, it is no longer a path but has become something else.

HIKING
TRAILS

S CIENCE DESCRIBES MORE than a million and a half different living species in nature. There are perhaps tens of millions more that have not yet been discovered, but most birds and terrestrial vertebrates have been registered and described. Among these, one stands out when it comes to movement and migration.

The little arctic tern covers more distance throughout its life than any other living creature. It is a beautiful bird. Compared to gulls, its body is rather small. It has a red beak, a black cap, and a gleaming white aerodynamic body. If you are watching an arctic tern for the first time, it won't take long to realize that here is a bird that can fly with the least effort imaginable, and is thus able to fly over very long distances. The arctic tern migrates between the northernmost and southernmost tips of the globe, back and forth, twenty-five thousand miles every year, on paths in the sky, the same air currents that have blown for generations. Something inherent in the arctic tern drives it to do this, and this act of relocation and navigation is at the core of its life. The arctic tern does not fly from the North Pole to the South Pole and back again merely to add a little spice to its day. It does it because it must.

It's the same with wild reindeer and sheep. No one can make paths quite the way they do. They have mastered the art of the path, but they don't create these paths out of a desire to walk; they create them because that's simply what you do if you're a reindeer or a sheep.

The eel migrates from the Sargasso Sea off the coast of Mexico all the way to Europe, where it then goes ashore and crosses through damp grass under the cover of nightfall until it reaches small ponds and lakes in inland Norway. The eel follows its own underwater paths, ocean currents that allow small newborn fry to zip around and speedier routes that individual adults use to reach their destinations simply and efficiently. The eel migrates, but it sets off on its adventurous journey neither for the sake of exercise nor to explore new submarine landscapes.

HUMANS ARE THE only beings that walk for the sake of walking, and for this purpose we have created specially adapted paths, or trails. In our day and age, hiking trails dominate the landscape and they exist in countless variations and forms. Some are intended for the sole purpose of hiking. Others are cultural trails, wildlife trails, or historical paths upon which, in addition to the hike itself, the intention is to learn something along the way. Some hiking trails follow ancient pilgrimage and trade routes. They are marked with signs and adapted to those who are driven on their journey either by religion or more worldly ambitions. Long-distance trails were created for those who wish to challenge themselves physically and mentally. Some long-distance trails even stretch for thousands of miles and take several months to walk from beginning to end.

Personally, I tend to walk somewhere between fifteen hundred and two thousand miles each year. As the crow flies, that is roughly the distance from Oslo to Rome, or from Atlanta, Georgia, to Portland, Oregon. But the distance I cover is broken up into hundreds of smaller stages and I rarely walk more than twelve to eighteen miles in a single day.

I walk long distances, but I always wish I could keep on going. I would love to leave everything behind me and just walk, day after day, for thousands of miles, on paths I've never taken before and toward places I've never seen. Maybe one day I will set out on such a trip, maybe not. For the time being, I satisfy myself by talking with people who have covered enormous distances on foot over weeks and months on trails. And all of them say the same thing about it: you enter into an inner state that you have never been in before and from which, after awhile, you never wish to emerge. Your relationship to the path becomes so intense and emotional that it is eventually difficult to imagine a full and valuable life anywhere other than on the trail, and doing anything other than walking.

MY FRIENDS VIBEKE Fürst Haugen and Agnete Brun hiked the Camino de Santiago in Spain, an ancient pilgrimage route that has now been adapted for tourists. They began in Saint-Jean-Pied-de-Port on the French side of the Pyrenees. From there, they set off to follow the trail nearly five hundred miles to the famous cathedral at Santiago de Compostela in Spain. The journey was a completely new experience for both of them: neither woman had ever hiked such a long distance before, and this probably explains why they decided to average a pace of four miles an hour. Walking at a speed of four miles per hour is very fast. And if you plan to cover a distance of nearly five hundred miles, you need to be in relatively good shape and have good endurance. The two friends planned to spend five weeks on the trail, walking for six days in a row and taking every seventh day off to rest.

Santiago de Compostela is a small city in northwestern Spain. The city's cathedral is a renowned pilgrim destination for European Catholics because a grave purportedly belonging to the apostle James was uncovered there in AD 813. James was executed in AD 44, and the story goes that his body was brought to Compostela, where his remains were interred and a church built over the grave. In AD 1000, the original church was replaced by the imposing cathedral that stands there now and that is the ultimate destination for pilgrims walking the trail.

The friends began to walk, and as they did, they started to realize that life along the trail was different than they had expected. It was larger and more powerful. They began to understand that they were part of a community, that they were walking on a path and toward a goal that was more than just a geographical point. Their trek was larger than themselves: it was not only a hike along a physical path, it was also an inner journey.

As they neared Santiago de Compostela, one of them wrote in her journal:

I have begun to view the pilgrimage as a living organism, as a train that has been moving for hundreds of years—and that will continue to move forever. We have lived life along the camino for these past four weeks. That has been our job. Now it will soon be over. Others will take up where we leave off and the organism will continue to live without us.

And the other wrote:

I had a powerful sense of being at one with myself. I knew that I was able to cover great distances without any problem, to get up in the morning and walk to the ends of the earth. We walked and we didn't require anything else. Not only was this a strong feeling of freedom, it was also a feeling of safety.

Both friends came to realize that walking over long distances and spans of time is the surest way to find oneself. You repeat the same activity day after day. Walk, walk, walk. You feel the blood pulse in your veins, course throughout your body; you become attuned to your body's own rhythms. You become one with yourself and everything around you.

We left El Burgo Ranero at dawn when the sun was low. I desire nothing more than what I have here.

*My legs, the sun, the air, my backpack, life, the birds,
the flowers, the path, and the goal.*

On May 26, their journey came to an end. It was
a Sunday. They walked the last steps up the old stone
stairs to the cathedral in Santiago de Compostela. The
stairs were curved, worn down by all the feet that had
trod there before them.

*The camino is a trail full of sorrow and joy and for-
giveness. And the need still remains. We continue to
struggle with ourselves, just as everyone has done
before us. "Sorrow" and "forgiveness": for me, these
two words became synonymous with life along the trail.
The pilgrimage is a fellowship. Young people walk in
the footsteps of the old, and the needs are the same
today as they were when the trail was walked for the
first time.*

In a certain sense, the wildlife trails, historical paths,
and cultural trails are the opposite of natural paths.
Although hiking trails often follow the route of older
paths, they are by contrast planned, designed, and
altered. Behind a hiking path is deliberate thought;
it results not as a natural consequence of collective
movement but rather as an act of will by one or several

determined individuals. The hiking path is universal in its form, clearly marked, and accessible for all. Before you even start hiking, it's easy to gather relevant information about the trail, such as its level of difficulty, landmarks, distance, and the estimated time to walk its full length.

In Norway where I live, the first marked hiking trail was created in 1874 and was signposted by a large letter T on rocks, trees, or signs along the way. The trail was built upon a route in central Norway that led from the Sjodalen valley and up over the Besseggen mountain ridge. The Norwegian Trekking Association had been founded seven years prior, and this historic moment represented the start of the Norwegian philosophy of *friluftsliv*. Translated as "fresh air life" or "outdoor life," this approach to spending time outdoors for physical and spiritual well-being is still an integral part of people's lives today. The idea has even enjoyed some recent attention outside of Norway, as books about Scandinavian approaches to health and happiness have become international bestsellers. However, in the second half of the 1800s in Norway, friluftsliv appealed first and foremost to the bourgeoisie who needed fresh air, unspoiled nature, and a welcome pause from their hectic urban lives. People in the lower classes had more than enough to do just to make ends meet. For them,

life was all about work and enjoying free time in the great outdoors was an unfamiliar concept.

Since 1874, the Norwegian Trekking Association has blazed and maintained trails enjoyed by hikers visiting from around the globe. The association is now responsible for more than thirteen thousand miles of marked summer trails in the country, a distance equal to half the earth's circumference.

+

AS MY VISIT with my father came to an end, I asked if I could borrow the photo of my sisters and me on the path behind the cabin. I brought it back to Oslo with me and put it in a book so it wouldn't get bent. I took it out often to look at it, and each time I did I experienced the same sensation of traveling back in time.

The spring got warmer and greener, and soon winter was no more than a distant memory. It was time for summer vacation. My partner and I took our children to our usual vacation spot on Kråkerøy, an island across from the city of Fredrikstad, just south of Oslo. We did what families always do when vacationing at the seaside. We swam, barbecued, entertained guests, visited others, drank wine, ate ice cream, and went for short walks. After several weeks of leisure, I decided it was

time to take a longer walk. I couldn't drive, so I had to choose the nearest possible path. Fortunately, the closest path picked up right outside our cabin door.

That path is a coastal path, and it circumnavigates the entire island of Kråkerøy. It is roughly twenty miles long, and it is marked by either small metal signs affixed to trees or by blue paint on stones. You'd have to be extremely bad at following signs to get lost on this coastal path.

Strangely enough, I had never walked this path before, so while the rest of the family was busy eating their breakfast and preparing for a long day at the beach, I packed a light backpack, pulled on some shorts and tennis shoes, and set off.

Kråkerøy covers an area of seven-and-a-half square miles. Because the coastal path goes in a loop around the island, it has neither a beginning nor an end and you can choose to join it and take off at any point. All you have to do to walk the entire distance is keep going until you return to where you started.

I ambled along at a leisurely pace, pausing along the way, taking photos, studying the landscape: the cabins and the sea, the birds and the fields. At the south end of Kråkerøy is a dark gray metal suspension bridge leading to a cluster of islands that make up Ytre Hvaler National Park. Next to this looming bridge, whose two futuristic clothespin-shaped concrete towers are connected by black cables stretched out like arms, the GPS on my cell phone indicated I had reached the halfway mark. I rewarded myself with a lunch break, and while I ate I flipped through the photos on my camera. Each one was a variation on the topic "coastal path," and together they documented a wide diversity of natural habitats and cultural landscapes: smooth bedrock outcroppings, open pine forests, small boat landings, marshes and bird sanctuaries, dense clusters of deciduous trees, green fields and yellow fields, farms with red barns and white farmhouses.

I finished eating and continued my walk. Since I was now at the southernmost point of the island, I guessed the path would soon change direction and after a brief stretch it did, veering northeast into dark coniferous forests with tall trees that swayed unnervingly in the fresh summer wind.

My tennis shoes and the dry dirt of the path made for easy walking. There was hardly anything in my pack, and with every step I became more and more enthusiastic about hiking trails in general and coastal paths in particular.

If the natural path is the most expedient way between two points, hiking trails are the most beautiful. Their purpose is not practical; it's aesthetic. Such

sleep. Every day she woke at five in the morning, ate breakfast, repacked her gear, and began to walk. For a thousand miles she repeated this routine, covering twenty miles a day for fifty-three days on the same trail, and this is why I wanted to talk with her.

What she told me echoed a description by my two friends who had undertaken the pilgrimage to Santiago de Compostela. The terrain they passed through couldn't have been more different—my two friends walking across the cultural landscape of France and Spain and Anette hiking through barren wilderness on the western frontier of the US—but their experiences, and their relationship to the path as they moved, were strikingly similar. Anette said:

> I found myself outside of everything; there was nothing but me and the landscape. I walked and walked and I was in a constant flow, as if I were meditating for hours a day. During the first four weeks, I was so sore, blister upon blister upon blister, but then it got better, and I thought, Walk, walk, walk: this is the life.
>
> The path meant everything; it was the thing I stared at all day long. Some days it was covered with snow. Other days there wasn't a trail at all, and on other days it was only made of rocks all day long. My feet were ruined, I hated the path intensely, and I

thought: Damn path! I can't take it anymore! *But then there were days when the path was wide and flat and there were no rocks. Then those of us who were hiking it would say to each other: "The trail is kind to us today."*

Long-distance trails too are created and maintained only because someone takes care of them. Communities of volunteers across the globe devote an enormous amount of time and energy to them. Often called trail crews, they work without pay on various sections of these trails.

In Europe, a network of twelve long-distance trails has been developed to traverse the continent. Referred to as the E-Paths, these signed routes make it possible to hike from one path to another in succession, to cover vast distances.

Hiking trails like these are everywhere, crisscrossing every type of terrain and representing every variation of length and difficulty. The Shikoku Henro trail in Japan. The Inca trail to Machu Picchu in Peru. The Overland Track in Tasmania. The Tour du Mont Blanc in Switzerland, France, and Italy. The W Trek in Chilean Patagonia. The Rongai Route to the top of Mount Kilimanjaro. The Great Ocean Walk in Australia. The GR20 on Corsica.

El Caminito del Rey in Andalucia, Spain, is considered one of the most dangerous paths in the world. The trail runs along a platform attached in midair on a sheer cliff face and it has been closed until recently because many people fell to their deaths from the deteriorated walkway, and an even higher number sustained serious injuries. Not long ago, however, the trail was restored and it is once again open for brave hikers. Glass floor panels have been added along sections of the trail to give hikers the heightened feeling of being suspended in midair. When it comes to modern trail-blazing, El Caminito del Rey is in a class entirely of its own.

The world's most dangerous, oldest, most breathtaking—even in the world of hiking trails, it's important to stand out. Until recently, the Appalachian Trail in the United States was considered the world's longest hiking trail at 2,190 miles. But that record has now been surpassed by the Great Trail in Canada, a long-distance route that was known as the Trans Canada Trail until 2016 and made possible by the force of incredible volunteer service spanning several decades. The newly opened trail traverses the continent from coast to coast for over fifteen thousand miles.

HIKING TRAILS ARE put down by people for people, and foremost among these trail builders are the

Sherpas, mountain people in the Himalayas who build stairs and carry stones up thousands of feet so that hikers can reach their goal more safely and easily.

Of course, the downside of trail creation is that it opens up the landscape to more people, and the increased damage to nature is not insignificant. Such is the situation at the spectacular trail on Besseggen ridge in Norway. This beloved narrow mountain formation in Jotunheimen National Park plunges hundreds of feet on both sides of the trail to alpine waters below. Besseggen is a natural wonder, and over fifty thousand hikers cross the ridge every summer. As a result, the trail has become wider, deeply grooved, and clearly delineated. The well-trodden route has left an enormous footprint on the wilderness that will remain visible for centuries to come, even if at some point the path is closed to hiking. Countless such examples exist all around the world, and they remind us that even hiking trails can intrude upon and harm the landscape if they are traveled by too many people.

Only a few years ago, the trail between the Cinque Terre, five UNESCO-designated seaside villages in Italy, was closed due to the threat of landslides. Too many people were hiking the trail, which was not built to withstand such throngs. Sections of the trail are still closed while it is being restored and upgraded.

I myself hiked the Sentiero Azzurro, as this coastal trail is called, many years ago. It cuts into a steep cliff alongside a gorgeous landscape of olive groves and vineyards and citrus trees, with views over the Ligurian Sea, as it heads north from the village of Monterosso, via Vernazza, Corniglia, and finally, Manarola to Riomaggiore. At the time I walked the Cinque Terre, the trail had not yet been discovered by mass tourism. Hardly anyone was walking the trail, and the only people we encountered were local Italians heading to one of the neighboring villages to run an errand. These days, the local authorities estimate around a million and a half visitors per year.

✦

LIFE ALONG THE Kråkerøy coastal path that day was simple. I was alone but I didn't miss anyone—neither my partner nor our children. They were off swimming and eating ice cream and fishing. I was hiking the trail.

That summer day was as summer days should be. A lightness covered the landscape, leaving no room on the trail for dark thoughts. The sun beamed. Hours passed, and for every mile I put behind me, my mood buoyed. I was liberated from heavy boots and a heavy pack. I carried only the things I normally bring as part of my daily routine, even to the office: light clothes, a small bag of food, a water bottle, and an extra layer.

I passed oat fields that were still green. Swallows caught insects in the soft afternoon sunlight, and from the leafy trees the chaffinches and robins twittered. I unfolded my map to see where I was. Because I was following a clearly marked path, I had not checked the map for hours; there was no need. The map was a "cultural-historical hiking map." It highlighted the route but also small or significant points of interest along the path, places having to do with nature, culture, and history. I read about the glacial potholes and ancient trees. About Bjølstad Farm, where the Norwegian artist Edvard Munch's grandfather grew up. About the Åsgårdvarden, a tumulus, or burial mound, dating back to the Bronze Age and rising 120 feet above sea level. About Huth Fort, built in 1788, and about the Fastings Bastion, a defense for three cannons built in 1807.

The trail continued on through a sparse, light-filled pine forest. My body was as weightless as a balloon; my head was free of any worries. I trod softly along the trail, kept watch for some of the many roe deer that inhabit the island. Then I heard the buzzing sound of a lawn mower and soon after that I found myself in a residential area with people roaming around in their gardens, vacation-dazed. That's how it is with coastal trails: they are a journey in and out of civilization and nature. You might chance upon a deer at any moment. You might suddenly come upon people, cabins, convenience stores, cows, tractors, lawn mowers, and cars. When walking on coastal trails, it's best to be prepared for anything.

As I got closer to the mainland-side of the island, the development became more and more dense. From this point on, there will be nothing but asphalt, I thought, but then the path was swallowed up in a little grove of tall, skinny trees with green canopies that filtered the low evening sun and tossed trembling flecks of light onto the dark forest floor. Behind the trees, I could make out the towering cranes from an old abandoned shipyard. It was almost touching to think how the people who created this trail had pressed it into the trees wherever possible, regardless of how sparse the trees might be.

It was only when I started on the final leg back to the cabin that I realized how tired I was. I had been walking for over eighteen miles. My feet were sore. And yet I also knew that I would be in a fantastic mood for the rest of the day—easygoing, mild, and patient. I could play with the children for hours, cook dinner, tidy up the cabin, smile and laugh, the sole reason being the trail and having walked on it. I didn't need anything else, and in this simple fact lies an important truth: we have an inherent urge to wander that we seldom think about but that we are reminded of every time we follow a path.

+

I CONTINUED TO go walking for the rest of the summer vacation. Because I couldn't drive, every day I did my grocery shopping on foot. I took my biggest backpack and hiked the four miles to the store. Once there, I filled the backpack with groceries and walked back again. It took three hours from the time I left the cabin until I returned, but my absence hardly seemed noticed.

They only started gawking when I began to walk barefoot. I decided to take off my shoes and put them into a closet, and there they stayed for the rest of the vacation. On bare feet I walked across warm bedrock outcroppings and through knee-high blueberry bushes, on soft paths and hard gravel roads. I walked shoeless up the mountain, hobbling over the plateau in my hobbit-feet. I went to visit other people barefoot. I went to the grocery store without shoes on. The floor of the grocery store was cold and flat. It was so hard I could feel the way the jolt from my heel reverberated up my spine and all the way to my head each time my foot hit the floor, a sensation I never feel when walking along uneven terrain with natural elements underfoot. One day a little boy was shopping with his dad. When he saw me, he stopped and yelled: "Look at that man, Daddy, he's not wearing shoes!"

I loved it. Shoes and socks belonged to another era. I had become a Stone Age man; yes, I had become the island's last remaining specimen of *Homo erectus*. My feet got brown and flat. They were almost certainly several sizes bigger than they had been at the start of the summer. The skin on my feet became chapped and as hard as an elephant's skin. My toes started to look more deformed than they usually do, and the soles of my feet resembled a cropped aerial photograph of an African savannah that hadn't received rain for many years.

On one of the final days of our vacation, my friend John and his family paid us a visit. And one evening, John and I hatched a plan, which is what happens every time we get together. At some point in the visit, we inevitably start talking about going backpacking together, and this evening was no different. We pored over maps and discussed different possibilities, and by the time we waved goodbye to John and his family the next day, the details for our expedition had been laid.

A few days later, our summer holiday came to an end. We packed our things and prepared to return to the city. I unwillingly pulled on socks and shoes once more. The sensation was extremely uncomfortable, restrictive, and claustrophobic. Anyone who has gone barefoot for an entire summer will know what I mean. The shoes felt stiff. The socks itched infernally. I felt very sorry for my feet. I thought of them as two free souls taken hostage and forced into separate confined prison cells, not to be released until a whole year had passed and it was summer once more.

THE TREK
OVER THE HIGH
MOUNTAIN

—————

ONE BRISK AND blustery late summer's day, I found myself a new path. The landscape had changed in appearance from the weeks prior. Evenings were filled with the intense chirping of grasshoppers, and in the mornings the artificial light fixtures were plastered with insects of every shape and size. The world was no longer the color of chlorophyll. The all-encompassing green color had shifted to yellow and red and orange. The grass was drier; blueberries and cranberries had popped up.

I stood on a moraine ridge on a high mountain plateau with a view across a large lake. With me were five companions, one large and four small: my good friend John, his children, and my own. Two eleven-year-old girls and two nine-year-old boys. We were ready to carry out the plan we had hatched on Kråkerøy a few weeks earlier, and the children were surprised and delighted to have been included. Before us were forty-five miles of hiking over the high mountains of the Hardanger Plateau in central Norway between Oslo and Bergen. We would be walking on and off trails for long stretches each day. John and I were excited. The children were excited too, they said, but I wasn't sure if they knew quite what they were facing.

We stood on the moraine ridge for a particular reason. We were searching for a set of ancient, overgrown tracks, a path that crosses this section of mountains from east to west. Large portions of it have long been erased, but there are still visible patches of it every now and then. The trail is one of the Nordmannsslepene, the Nordic tracks, and it was used by humans for thousands of years. *Nordmann* means "Nordic peoples" and *slepe* refers to the act of tugging or hauling something, in this case most likely a hand-pulled cart or sled. The path provided a safe passage across the windswept mountains, to the extent that travel over a mountain can be safe.

FROM THE RIDGE, we gazed over the big lake and down to the outlet of one of Norway's largest rivers, the Numesdalslågen. From its source, the river flows down from the mountain, through valleys, heading south toward the ocean. The river chooses the path of least resistance and runs effortlessly through the land- scape, as a walking path would do.

In order to reach our current location, we had taken a ferry across the lake and followed a marked trail from the lake north through a birch forest. We had climbed above the tree line, spent a night in tents, and contin- ued across the plateau, following in the footsteps of all the people who had gone before us. The trail we followed was covered with dirt and sand and pebbles and was grooved between heather and willow shrubs, which made it more difficult to walk. It was worn into the landscape, so deep it was impossible to miss. Whenever the path crossed a stony part of the moun- tain where it was impossible for a groove to form, it was marked instead by a cairn or a letter T painted in red on a rock to keep hikers from going astray.

After a long day's trek, we arrived at the Lågaros alpine hut, a humble wooden building erected by the Norwegian Trekking Association in 1960. We decided to spend the night there. We got a room and ate dinner in the common room. As we ate, we talked with other hikers. The conversations were about trails, only trails, nothing but trails. Everyone talked about their own trail and asked others about theirs. "It was a glorious day, wasn't it?" "Cold and wet but that doesn't matter." "There's no such thing as bad weather, only bad clothes." "Where are you from, which trail did you take?" "Was it dry, wet, steep, flat, wide, narrow?" "Where are you headed tomorrow, which trail are you going to take?"

As the afternoon and evening wore on, more hikers arrived. They ate, dried their clothes over the woodstove, lounged about in the common room and launched into conversations about trails. There was every manner of person: business leaders, shop employees, anesthetists, and child welfare workers. In this simple hut, we were all alike, happy that we had just been hiking on a trail all day long and content in the knowledge that we would do it again the next day.

When the discussions about trails finally ebbed, everyone went to bed. The snoring of hikers was so loud it rattled the flimsy wood-paneled walls. We got up early the next day, because there are advantages to being a type-A personality when hiking. We ate breakfast in the common room, and as we ate we picked up our conversations about trails. But now the discussion was no longer about which trails we took yesterday, but rather which trails we were going to take today.

After breakfast had been devoured, the other hikers said their goodbyes and have-a-nice-hikes. And then they were off, scattered in every direction on different paths. Minutes later, the hut was empty. It would remain like that until late afternoon, when it would once again fill with new hikers drying their clothes over the woodstove and lounging about the common room talking about trails.

We packed our knapsacks too. The children were rested and happy about finding themselves in such a strange place, a spot exotic in its simplicity for little people growing up in the 2000s. They explored every cranny of the little hut, every tiny nook, and so it took John and me some time to gather the troops. We were the last of the overnight guests to leave the hut. The wind rang in our ears and the children ran whooping across the high mountain with their tiny backpacks.

WE LEFT THE moraine ridge with the view over the lake and river and followed a trail eastward. I kept watch for the ancient Nordic tracks. Although I could not see them, I was convinced they would appear sooner or later.

Among forests and cultural landscapes with deep, fertile soil, paths vanish quickly if they are not in constant use. They become overgrown. The ground is covered up with grass and ferns and moss and flowers, and even the opening in the trees disappears because branches always stretch toward the most sunlight. Up on the tundra-like highlands, it's a different story. There is no tall growth at these altitudes; there's nothing but heather and lichen and willow brush. The earth is barren, and the bedrock is often only a quarter of an inch or so beneath the heather. In a landscape like this, it can take hundreds of years for a trail to be fully erased. The process is very slow, which is why such landscapes are particularly vulnerable to human encroachment.

The Nordic tracks were listed as historical trade routes by the Cultural Heritage Act of 1979. The two main tracks are the Great and the Southern Nordic Tracks, but an entire network of paths leads every which way among the mountains up here, with offshoots leading to long valleys like the small secondary roads that break off our modern highways. These offshoots reveal the ways in which people have diverged as they've walked through the mountains. Some traversed east to west, others from south to north. These foot travelers represented every walk of life and every region: bishops from Stavanger, farmers from the great eastern valleys, landscape painters from Bergen, academics from Oslo, fishermen from the south, and government officials from Nidaros.

Some parts of the Nordic tracks are still visible today on the Hardanger Plateau and these spots are well known and marked by the easily recognizable red T. One route is known as the Great Nordic Track. This trail starts along a fjord and climbs steeply up to the highlands. From this point on the plateau, it crosses the entire wide-open expanse until it ends back down in the valley.

We had planned our trip such that we would end up at another hut in the town of Mårbu. If you follow the marked trail, the distance between our start and end point is a normal day trip. We could have followed this trail, of course, but John and I wanted to do something different. We wanted to try to find the ancient tracks in those places where they were not well marked or maintained as modern trails are, but rather only existed as remnants of something foregone, the last visible signs of travel almost completely wiped out, now only remembered by old hand-drawn maps and stories from a different time.

HARDANGER PLATEAU IS northern Europe's highest continuous mountain plateau, towering an average of over thirty-six hundred feet above sea level. The plateau is like a lid atop southern Norway: flat, lofty, and grand. Although it spans the vast interior of the country, no one lives there. People inhabit the valleys and the coasts in every direction, so originally those who wanted to contact others in nearby towns and cities were obliged to cross the plateau. It is considered an inhospitable terrain, desolate and windy and ice cold, with waist-high snowdrifts in the winter. This landscape hasn't changed since the first hunter-gatherers arrived in the Stone Age in pursuit of wild reindeer, the primitive creature of Norwegian fauna that still exists today.

We hiked east. The sweeping vistas took our breath away; it felt like we were looking out onto the vast expanse of an ocean. We saw bulging hills like waves in hues of sun and shadow. They were yellow and green where the sunlight illuminated them, and gray and almost black where it did not reach. Everywhere, covering the dark mountains and the wide plains, we saw lichen—the main food source for the wild reindeer that brought humans to Norway in the first place.

The sky grew darker. The wind grew more relentless. We passed a shelter made of flat stone slabs, one of many such shelters on the Hardanger Plateau. Some of these stone shelters have been restored by Norway's Travel Association or equipped by one of the local mountaineering groups with bunkbeds and heating and cooking facilities. Others remain as rudimentary as they were when first erected, with no comforts other than providing cover from the wind and weather.

The children roved every which way, like bird dogs on a grouse hunt. If everyone moved in the manner of children, there would be no such thing as paths. Two pairs of feet would never touch the same spot, and this is what the Norwegian philosopher Arne Næss had in mind every time he hiked to his mountaintop cabin, Tvergastein, in southern Norway. Næss deliberately followed a different route to his cabin every time he went because he never wanted to create a path leading there.

As I observed the chaotic rambling of our children over the plateau, I was reminded of the first time I took my son on an overnight camping trip in a tent. He was four years old. We followed a path into the woods and slept near a small pond. My son walked ahead of me, and I walked behind and studied him. He darted off-course constantly, clambering up boulders, gathering pinecones, trying to pull up large trees by their roots. Not only didn't he stay on the trail, he barely even noticed it. He had no concept of distance, no ability to allocate his energy. When he felt strong, he ran. When he got exhausted, he lay down on the ground.

THE DISTINCTIVE LANDSCAPE of the Hardanger Plateau unfolded before us, undulating like an endless, unmoving sea. The ground was a mosaic of tufted reindeer moss, crimson heather, and slender cotton grass.

Gravel and sand. Flat stones covered by green map lichen. We turned to head southeast and had the wind at our backs. It was a powerful wind that pushed us forward, and the children wondered why it had suddenly become so much easier to walk.

I was still looking for the ancient tracks. I swept my gaze over the landscape, back and forth, back and forth. We walked along a lake and passed a steep cliff with an enormous and very visible vertical crack. The crack was two yards wide and thirty feet high. It was located above us, with its opening facing east. John said he would like to examine the crack to see whether he could find evidence of humans. He climbed up. I stood watching him, thinking that he was doing exactly what the first person to have passed here long ago must have done. First that traveler noticed the crack in the cliff and then, without a second thought, was pulled in to investigate further whether it might be a good shelter from the wind and bad weather, and thus a life-saving spot in a pinch.

John returned.

It wasn't exactly a cave he had found, he reported, but a hole with enough space for two people to fit inside. It wasn't unlikely that someone might have sought refuge here at some point, and we wondered whether this might mean we were closer to the old tracks than we knew?

It made sense to us that such spots of shelter might be close to the ancient trails, or that the trails would pass close to possible shelters. This is where travelers might have spent the night during their climb over the mountain or perhaps where they huddled away from a storm or heavy rain. The crack in the cliff was a sign. We heightened our attention and fixed our eyes on the ground ahead of us. Not long afterward, John called out—and I must reluctantly admit it is always John who discovers things:

"Here they are. Here are the tracks!"

There were visible marks in the soil, two tracks running in parallel with four to five feet between them. The tracks were four inches deep, twelve inches wide, and half covered by grass and lichen. There was no doubt that these were indeed the ancient Nordic tracks. I stood looking at them and was filled with a sense of smallness and awe. These ancient paths represent a link between the past and the present. They have traversed the Hardanger Plateau for thousands of years, possibly even as far back as eighty-five hundred years ago. Some theories suggest humans created them, while others believe they were old animal tracks carved by reindeer, sheep, and horses. Where the trails are wide, they could indicate traces of large reindeer herds. Where they are narrower, they may have been made by the hooves of sheep or horses—animals that walk in a row one by one.

I felt suddenly happy and relieved that we had managed to fulfill our self-imposed mission. It felt like we had uncovered a secret of significance to the entire human race, an artifact from the cellar of history that had been brought up into daylight and dusted off by six sharp and fearless explorers. We called for the children and showed them the tracks. They looked with disinterest at the ground before running off again.

We kept heading east on the tracks we had found. The trail became impossible to see and seemed to vanish in places but then it would reappear. These tracks followed the same direction we intended to go, and if we trusted the old maps we had studied, they would connect us to the marked hiking trail leading to the Mårbu hut and the end of our journey. We explained this to the children, but they were more occupied with sneaking up on some ptarmigans that had just flown up from a thicket of willow shrubs a hundred yards ahead. The children realized they would need weapons to catch the ptarmigans. They searched for sticks to use as spears. But they quickly realized we were above the tree line and thus there were no sticks for miles around. John and I watched them. I noted the same behavior I had earlier observed when John went to examine the crack in the cliff. The children collected rocks, crouched, and slowly began creeping toward the birds.

John and I stood in the grooves of the ancient tracks, following them with our eyes, those four living beings who were proof that the hunting instinct has evolved less since the Stone Ages than we might like to think.

THE AFTERNOON CAME. The reindeer moss glowed white and pale green, a color reminiscent of the clock hands on old wristwatches. The low, late-summer sun cast long shadows ahead of us and highlighted the tracks like black streaks across a white page.

We found a good camping spot on the shore of a lake and pitched our tents. Evening came, and then night. And then it was morning, and when we pulled down the zipper and peered outside we were looking east, where the ancient tracks continued below a vast blue sky.

✦

SHEEP ARE THE foremost pathfinders of the high mountains. On our hike, we constantly came across small flocks. They did not seem to be moving according to any plan or along a path, but we knew they were. The sheep observed us as an interesting break to their monotonous daily routine but kept their distance. A long summer in the highlands had made them wary of people. Perhaps they had forgotten they usually lived among people, but autumn was approaching and soon their owner would come to lead them down to the valley and into the barn. There they would stand throughout the winter until they were led out again along the trails up into the mountains. At that point, perhaps they would have forgotten the mountain existed, just as they had now forgotten about humans.

After a while, the Nordic tracks disappeared again and did not reappear. We no longer had a trail to follow, but we had markers. Rock cairns were piled strategically along the terrain, their relief always visible against the sky.

Cairns are directional markers that blend in with the landscape the way paths do. These piles of rocks are nearly imperceptible adjustments that make it easier to find one's way. The Norwegian word for "cairn," *varde*, comes from the Old Norse word *varði*, which means "attentiveness" or "vigilance." The English word "cairn" means "heap of rocks." In Norway, cairns have historically been used to mark borderlines and trigonometric points used for creating maps. They were built near the sea in order to clearly signal special points along a shipping line and they were used in the mountains to show the way. Many of the cairns on the Hardanger Plateau are new, piled there by the Norwegian Trekking

Association. It's nice the organization has chosen to use this age-old form of trail marker and to build it in the same way it always has been.

Up on the Hardanger Plateau, the cairns vary in form, size, and age. The oldest may be several thousand years old. The Norwegian geologist Christopher Hansteen mentioned the cairns when writing about a trip he took in 1821. He called them "comforting guides."

> These enormous rock masses, of which one can see perhaps fifty in an outward circle around oneself, help to show the way through this wilderness without the use of a compass. In addition to the largest of these, wandering souls have stacked two to three smaller stones in the direction one should walk, so that soon after passing one marker, one's eyes then fall upon the next.

We followed the cairns throughout the morning, late morning, and afternoon. We were hiking without a path, farther and farther to the east, and around about the time we thought we might be getting close to the modern hiking trail leading to the hut, we spotted other hikers walking in a row along a ridge on the other side of a wide prairie. They were the first people we had seen in two days. The children loved the sight of other people and they longed for a real trail. They sped up, gliding over the heather, and when we reached the spine of the ridge where they finally caught sight of the red T, they were happy and felt assured that we would be able to reach our goal at last.

We followed the trail down into the valley. We no longer had to concentrate on where we were going. We didn't have to read the landscape anymore; this landscape had already been read and interpreted by thousands of people before us. It began to rain. The mountains grew higher and pointier and soon the dwarf birch trees appeared. The wind slowed but the rain came down more heavily. Afternoon turned into evening. We pulled up the hoods of our jackets. We walked and walked. No one spoke; each person was deep in their own thoughts. The rhythm of walking, the rhythm that belongs to the trail alone, had finally overtaken us.

PART

II

THE PATH AS
I REMEMBER IT

———

CHILDREN HAVE A different relationship to paths than adults do. I remember the path behind my little childhood cabin as mysterious and enchanting. It was a way into an unknown landscape that, although it was familiar because I had been there many times before, nonetheless changed from time to time and from season to season.

The path changed as well. In the summer, it was encircled by flowers and wild strawberries. By late summer, the flowers were replaced by yellow straw that drooped heavily with dew and dampened my pants. In September, the mushrooms came up. And in October, the leaves fell off the trees and covered the path—yellow and red leaves that stuck to your boots and turned the path slick as soap. Then came the first frost. The landscape stiffened and the path crackled roughly under our boots.

In the winter, the path was covered with snow. It vanished then, and only the sharpest observer could guess the line that followed the stream and the opening between the snow-heavy branches of trees. It turned up again in the spring: first as a stream of ice-cold runoff from the snow, then as a dry streak in the earth, blanketed with the old yellow grass from the previous year and wreathed with white and blue wood anemones and lilies of the valley that smelled like hope.

I can still picture that path clearly after all these years. If I close my eyes and concentrate, I can still recall every inch of it, the way the fingers remember guitar strings, piano keys, or the key holes of a flute. It's like a rule learned by heart, impossible to forget.

We always started at the cabin. From there, we would walk across a little meadow and past the parakeet Jakob's grave, the bird that was in the old photo I'd seen at my father's kitchen table.

That's where the path began. On the right was a hillside flanked with deciduous trees. In the fall, you could see far up the slope, all the way to the top of the hill, but in the summer the only thing visible was an impenetrable wall of green leaves.

On the left were dense clusters of hazel trees, one of the first varieties of tree to colonize Norwegian soil after the last glacial period. We would build shelters in those trees every summer and feast on hazelnuts every fall. I can still remember the hazelnut's shell: it is white, almost soft. We would place the nuts on a large rock and smash them with a smaller rock. The blow required precision. If we stopped short applying force just before the stone smashed the nut, it would touch with the perfect impact and we could remove the nut whole from the shell. But if we followed through on the blow and did not check the movement in time, the nut would splinter like a bit of crushed porcelain and it would take us the rest of the day to pick the bits of nut from the shell. Hazelnuts were an important part of the diet of Stone Age humans, and they were an important part of ours. In those days, the word "tree" was synonymous with "hazel" in my mind, and I believed that the world was full of them.

When we passed the meadow with the hazel trees and the parakeet Jakob's grave, the path flattened out and continued under large spruce trees. This was a disquieting, scary place. The ground was dark and lifeless; the air was always cold. If it was warm outside, it would be less warm under the spruces. If it was cold out, it would be even colder in that place.

We tended to walk quickly through the dark forest, staring in beneath the heavy branches. We were worried some mythical creatures might pop out—wood nymphs, gnomes, trolls—but everything was empty and quiet, and when we finally emerged from the other side the landscape opened up. The path swung to the left, across wet soil that was swamp-like with small, scattered pools of water. We had to hop from tussock to tussock to keep from getting soaked, and I didn't know why but it was always moist in this place no matter how dry it was everywhere else.

The path joined an old forestry road and veered to the right. The road had been created by the person who had owned the big forest in the 1800s, and by the time I was a child it was so overgrown and indistinct you would never have noticed it if you didn't already know it was there. The path followed the same route and had become a path on top of an overgrown forestry road.

To the right of the path was a tall mountain. The side of the mountain rose vertically, fifteen to twenty feet straight up from the ground. Above this was a sharp, threatening overhang. It loomed over our heads like a dark menace from outer space, pale gray, smooth granite, flat like the polished stone wall behind a woodstove in an old house.

We hurried past the overhang so the mountain wouldn't fall on our heads, and every time we passed it, our mother would tell us a story from when she was a little girl. The story went that the horse pulling their wagon was always allowed to pause next to the mountain before they continued. The horse was hot after having come all the way from the farm, and a cooling breeze always blew in this very spot, she said. She told the story in a way that made it sound mysterious, like an adventure. A cooling breeze? We pricked up our senses, my sisters and I, but everything around us seemed quite ordinary. There was no breeze against the mountain on breezeless days. And if it did blow, the wind didn't seem like anything out of the ordinary.

After we had passed the mountain, only a few steps remained before the waterfall, and from there the path took a sharp upward turn. These final steps were a tribulation. The grass and wild strawberries disappeared, now there was nothing but gravel and rocks. The pebbles would roll under our feet, causing us to lose our footing and struggle to balance. It was a grueling stretch, but by then we were down to the final few yards and we could already hear the water roaring up ahead.

There was a bridge that crossed the waterfall. I cannot remember what the bridge was made of, whether it was built of flat rocks or round logs, but I remember that we would hang over the side and stare down into the frothing mass of water with its great shining bubbles, white foam, and dark, alarming swirls. We would throw sticks and pinecones into the rapids on the upper side of the bridge and then rush to the other side to watch them come sailing out and then flow rapidly downstream. It was the biggest waterfall I knew about, and it was also the only one.

AFTER THE WATERFALL, the path headed up toward the right. Then it flattened out again and was green and cheerful. The rocks and gravel were gone. Here the path was covered with grass and flowers and surrounded by thick, succulent straw. The terrain seemed to open up. We would see verdant meadows and flapping summer birds. We could hear the sound from a thousand buzzing insects.

We were getting closer to the field where my grandparents used to cut grass for their animals, but first we would have to cross the stream once more. The second bridge was crafted from logs. The stream flowed quietly, it gurgled and trickled, green grass swayed in the current, and the bottom was covered with pale stones that twinkled like gold in the sunlight. Primroses grew along the bank.

Streams and rivers are the only parts of nature that never rest, that never pause when evening falls. And running water, I could never get enough of it. I didn't realize it then, but there is a similarity between streams and paths. They are driven by the same logic. Streams plough effortlessly through the terrain. They don't follow a straight line; they don't follow the shortest distance or the quickest way. They follow the path of least resistance. Water seeks equilibrium, and it will continue to flow until equilibrium has been reached. Only then will it stop moving. A stream ceases to exist once it reaches the lake; a river stops running when it joins the ocean. When water arrives at its equilibrium point, it loses its speed and dissipates. The water disperses in every direction, and this is what a path does too, because the people who have walked it continue on beyond it, each in their own direction.

THE STREAM FLOWED in a large arc before swinging toward the right and down. Where it came from and where it ended up I did not know, and I didn't much care. It was enough that it was there, directly underfoot. At the time, I didn't understand that it was the same stream running under both bridges on the path. Such connections were too big and complex for me to imagine back then. I lacked the greater overview of the landscape; my young life was lived at ground level, and that was where my attention lay.

Once we had crossed over the second bridge, the path split in two. The path that veered to the right went over the top of a hill and down into a valley, but we never went that way.

Our path continued to the left, and after a short while we would arrive at the fields that were the reason for the path's existence. It was there that my grandma and grandpa rode with their horse and wagon to cut the grass with their scythes and hang it on racks. After the grass had dried, they would load it onto the wagon and wheel it down to the farm. There they would put it into a storage silo to keep it dry throughout the winter.

The field was where the path ended. Both children and adults had an unspoken agreement that once we reached the field, we would take a break. We drank juice from small plastic bottles and ate bread slices that had been wrapped in crinkly sandwich paper. My father gave us chocolate. He had been saving it to lure us all the way up.

Once the chocolate had been consumed, it was time to go back. We were still so small that we could have sat on our parents' shoulders all the way home, but the agreement between the children and adults contained a clause that meant anyone who got chocolate at the field also had to walk the entire way back. It was easy enough to agree to such conditions when we first stopped to take a break, but once the break was over and the chocolate was consumed, we immediately regretted it and wished we could declare that agreement null and void.

The sole comfort was that the return path led downhill. It was a different path than the one we had climbed. The uphill slog was now a downhill slope, and we saw the landscape from a different perspective. The second bridge across the stream became the first bridge across the stream. The mountain where the horse would rest was to our left. We hopped from tussock to tussock at the place where the ground was always wet. We entered the dark forest. We began to run, under the trees, out of the forest, into the light, past the parakeet Jakob's grave, across the final meadow, and all the way to the cabin steps.

We had done it, once again. Walked on our own two feet the entire way. Of course, we had complained when we made it halfway and the chocolate was gone, but who doesn't complain when their legs are sore and their body is heavy and warm? We would cheer and dance. We had reached the end of the path and we were now permitted to go inside the cabin, take off our boots, sink down onto the sofa, and resume our lives as sedentary beings.

✦

WHEN BILBO BAGGINS in J. R. R. Tolkien's *Lord of the Rings* trilogy finishes his autobiography after a long life of wandering, he gives the book a simple title: *There and Back Again*. I have always liked that title. It says nothing about what happened on the many adventures undertaken by Bilbo, whether they were good or bad, exhausting or pleasant, frightening or serene. The book's title refers only to the act of walking. He walked there. And then he turned around and walked back. And once he has finished his tale about himself and has punctuated it with one final period, he is back in his own living room where it all began. The ring is no more, the journey is over, and with it also life as he has known it.

INTO
THE WILD

I N T H E W E E K S that followed after John and I
returned from our hike along the ancient Nordic
tracks, I continued seeking out new paths I had never
taken, both in Oslo and beyond its limits. Summer
vacation was long since over. The children had started
school again and the adults had returned to their work.
I myself was a free man. I had an office, but no boss. I
could decide how much to work and for how long, and
this particular autumn I decided to give myself a lot of
time off to go walking. This is work too, I told myself,
since thoughts flow more freely when you are walking
than when you are sitting.

The paths changed throughout the fall season. The
landscape was no longer lush. The grass slowly turned

yellow and the individual blades were full of dew in the mornings, heavy drops that caused them to stoop with bent heads. There were fewer insects. The first mushrooms started to appear. Light tennis shoes were replaced with tall boots. Winter hats. Gloves. And then the first nights of frost.

SEPTEMBER MADE WAY for October, and when autumn was at its most magnificent peak, I took the train north and out of the city once more with my friend John. While hiking across the Hardanger Plateau earlier that summer, we had hatched a new plan, just as we had hatched a plan to cross the Hardanger Plateau during our summer vacation on Kråkerøy.

Like that plan, this new one was also simple. We would walk for three days through the Nordmarka forest close to Oslo. We would hike off-trail, without a GPS or compass, with only the sun as our guide. We wanted the chance to experience the opposite of what it's like to walk on a path. We wanted to hike where no other foot had ever fallen, and where we would be required to determine the path of least resistance—or at least attempt to—amid the confusion of undisturbed wilderness.

John and I have undertaken many expeditions together, and every time we have learned something new about what it means to travel through nature. The first time we hiked together we were in high school. Almost thirty years have passed since then. We were eighteen years old when we first launched a canoe out onto a large lake early in January, the middle of the harsh Norwegian winter, which is the least likely time of year for a canoe trip in subarctic regions unless you happen to be an Inuk.

It was evening when we pushed the canoe out into the water. The surface of the lake was as black as oil. Our canoe was yellow. It was old and unsteady, having been cast in fiberglass many years earlier. After launching the boat, we realized we had forgotten our paddles at home. We found two pieces of board that we hoped we could use. They were too short, neither of them being more than three feet long.

We paddled out onto the lake, John sitting in front and I in back. We weren't wearing life vests, and no one knew where we were. If the canoe had capsized, we would have drowned. A human can't last for more than a few minutes in water that is close to its freezing point, but eighteen-year-old boys don't think of such things. They have their whole life ahead of them, and the thought of losing it is inconceivable.

I knew the lake well. It was the same lake that bordered the farm where my mother was born. You could see the lake from the tiny cabin. Several years earlier, my grandfather had showed me the paths on the lake, because paths also exist on the water. When the rain fell and the surface was flat, clear tracks formed across the water. The tracks were darker than the rest of the surface, and they crossed each other in strange patterns. Grandpa called them paths. I don't know why he called them that, since no one was creating them and no one was traversing them.

John and I paddled across the lake. We saw the lights from the farm behind us, but up at the cabin everything was dark. On the opposite side of the lake, we could see the lights from the highway and from a small coastal village, but the village was more than five miles away and that was not where we were headed.

The canoe was full of unnecessary supplies—even a shotgun we'd brought along, borrowed for the occasion from my sister's boyfriend. We planned to go hunting the next day, though we hardly knew anything about weapons or what we might shoot at.

We paddled far out into the deep water, freezing but happy to be on an expedition. There was no other noise save for the sound of the wooden boards hitting the water and the drops that fell each time we lifted them out of the water to begin another stroke. After a while, an island appeared directly in front of our canoe. The island wasn't large, but it was tall, and we could glimpse scattered pine trees among the crags. The ground was covered with a thick carpet of bilberry shrubs.

John suggested we spend the night on the island. We were frozen stiff, and neither of us could stand the thought of paddling any farther. We found a good spot up next to a rocky outcrop in the middle of the island, as far away from the water as possible. We had learned enough to know that the closer you are to open water in the winter, the colder the temperature tends to be.

We built a fire and drank whiskey. I don't think either of us had started liking whiskey at that point, but we drank it nonetheless. We had not brought a tent, so we unrolled our sleeping bags on the shrubs, directly on the ground, and I have never in my life spent a colder night. We had no clue about how to spend a night outside in the winter. Our sleeping pads were too thin. Our sleeping bags had been stored for years in tightly closed bags so the fibers had been permanently compressed and lost their insulating properties. There was not enough wood on the island to keep the fire going through the night.

The hunt was, of course, cancelled. We paddled back across the lake the next day in the dim morning light—a streak of gray across the eastern edge of the world. Neither of us spoke, but I think we both realized we were not the experienced wilderness explorers we had believed ourselves to be. Instead, we were complete amateurs.

I still have a photograph from that trip. It is faded now, bent at the corners. In the middle of the image, John is kneeling on the shrubs with the shotgun leaning on his right shoulder and the flask of whiskey in his hand. His face is pale and serious, lit up by the flash. He is wearing a black beret and gazing out at the winter sky. He is eighteen years old, in that phase of life in which humans have unlimited faith in their own abilities and are not interested in learning anything at all.

As we rode the train northward out of Oslo to begin our most recent adventure, John and I reminisced about that canoe trip. We were interrupted by a middle-aged man in an anorak, sitting directly opposite us. The man tilted his head when he noticed our backpacks, Gore-Tex clothing, and heavy boots. He asked if we were going on a hike. It was obvious we were going on a hike, but that didn't stop him from asking. We nodded in confirmation. The man wanted to know how far we were going to hike. Were we taking a tent, did we often go hiking, wasn't it cold now that it was autumn, which path were we planning to take?

The Nordmarka is a contiguous forest area that comprises over 106,000 acres. In our modern times it is an almost unheard-of privilege to have such a large wilderness area in close proximity to a European city. The Nordmarka is a classic boreal coniferous forest, a type of forest that only exists in subarctic climates and that stretches like a belt from North America via northern Europe and through to Siberia.

The Nordmarka forest has been a popular recreation area for hunters, fishers, and hikers since the mid-1800s. It was around this time that the Scandinavian philosophy of friluftsliv began to take hold in Norway. The concept, pronounced *free-loofts-leave*, has its roots in the nature-loving people of these northern countries, among whom are a large number of polar explorers. Friluftsliv implies love for, and connection with, nature through the regular practice of experiencing the freedom of the outdoors, often together with others. Toward the end of the 1800s, ski sports, particularly cross-country skiing, increased in popularity in Norway and city dwellers would often frequent the Nordmarka forest for winter activities.

The first ski map across this forest was drawn in 1890. Not only was it the first ski map of the area, it was also apparently the first such map in the world. The map was drawn by Ernst Bjerknes, a municipal planning officer in Oslo, which at the time was known as the city of Christiania. In his book *Via Skis, Velocipede and*

Sketchbook, Bjerknes describes how impassable and undiscovered the forest was at the time and therefore what a great need there was for paths and ski tracks:

> No one ever used to talk about clearing trails or marking ski tracks then.... This got me thinking that a ski map of the Nordmarka forest might be something useful... I went around from place to place and inquired about roads and paths that one might be able to take via skis.... Following these descriptions, I set off to discover passable tracks and to mark them down on the map with a red line. It was cumbersome but enjoyable work.

Bjerknes forged paths and marked them down on his map for the enjoyment of the public, and these still exist to this day. There are now paths crisscrossing the entire Nordmarka forest. The region is a vital green-space for many inhabitants from Oslo, hunters, fishers, hikers, and skiers.

A FEW MILES outside of the city limits, development began to thin, and not long after that we found ourselves in the countryside because that's how Oslo is situated. It's a European capital on the margins of the continent in a sparsely populated country with lots of open space.

Outside the train, the temperature was just above freezing. The autumn fog lay like a thick down blanket over the treetops. The deciduous trees gleamed in shades of red and yellow.

When we arrived at the station bordering the forest, we got off. From the platform, we gazed in to the Nordmarka forest, toward tall, fir-clad hills we knew we would have to cross before entering the heart of the forest. That was the gist of our plan: to reach the heart of the forest.

We bought bread, cold cuts, soup, and nuts at the local grocery store. Food that was light to carry but packed with energy. When we left the store, we repacked our gear and checked the map one final time. Then we folded it up and placed it at the bottom of a backpack together with our watches, cell phones, compass, and GPS. We weren't going to allow ourselves to take these out again until we had pitched camp the following evening. We were going to trust our own internal sense of direction for two days. I had already downloaded a GPS app on my phone that would not only give us our precise location when we finally checked it the next evening but that would also provide a detailed description of the direction we had walked, the time it took us, and the lines we had followed. Our goal was to walk in as straight a line as possible.

Before we buried the map in the backpack, we tried to memorize the terrain of the first few miles, and the direction and the elevation changes to the location we had selected as our goal for the first day. To our west was a ridge, about three to four miles away as the crow flies. This ridge was directly north of the city, so that if we could reach it before sundown, we would then be able to navigate south according to the sun on the following day. If we could manage this, we would eventually make our way back to the city.

A man was standing outside of the grocery store selling copies of the *War Cry*, the official magazine of the Salvation Army. He was an elderly man in a black uniform with red epaulettes. He wore a hat and a mild smile. I looked at him and at the pamphlet and realized he had committed himself to a life of spiritual discipline in the service of others.

THE STRAIGHT PATH. The narrow path. The path is a perfect metaphor. It can contain all of the emotions and longings in the world. Doubt and faith, birth and death, thoughts, hope, the road to salvation, the road into the unknown, the journey from beginning to end. The path shapes life itself or, in any case, life in the form of a Western Christian heritage in which life is a journey from birth to death, and human history is a journey from creation to Judgement Day.

We say of humans who have died that they have "departed," or that they've "taken their final journey." We "let our thoughts wander" and we "walk in some-one else's footsteps." "Hit the road," "trail off," "go off the beaten track": in every language, countless expres-sions draw from the concept of the path.

In his essay *Nature,* the American author and philos-opher Ralph Waldo Emerson writes:

> *Have mountains, and waves, and skies, no signifi-cance but what we consciously give them, when we employ them as emblems of our thoughts? The world is emblematic. Parts of speech are metaphors, because the whole of nature is a metaphor of the human mind.*

In fact, the metaphor of the path is used more fre-quently than the thing itself. If you do a Google search for the word "path," you will have to scroll through countless religious or spiritual references, pages about yoga, meditation, mindfulness, everything other than a physical path.

The Norwegian lumberjack and poet Hans Børli drew inspiration for his poetry from the woods where he worked and spent long portions of his life. In Børli's language, the path is both a metaphor and a concrete physical object. He has been called the poet of the forest and he must have had an intimate relationship to the forests in which he worked, because the word "path" appears in over seventy of his poems. For Børli, the path was not just a route from A to B; it was also a location and a link to the past.

The world's largest religions all make use of path metaphors. Hinduism has four paths to liberation. Buddhism has its eightfold path to peace and enlightenment. Judaism's term for its collection of religious law, halacha, originally means "way of walking." Of Islam's five pillars, the fifth and final rule (hajj) is a pilgrimage. In the Christian scriptures, Jesus says: "I am the way (the path), the truth, and the life."

The metaphorical implications of the path are obvious and easy to understand because, in a way, life is all about choosing the right way. This is what we struggle with on a daily basis, and it's what we try to teach our children. Everything boils down to making choices, being true to ourselves, and forging our own path. The path metaphors invite us to break with majority thinking. In the Bible (Matthew 7:14), it says: "But small is the gate and narrow the way that leads to life, and only a few find it."

This is the narrow way, and to take it requires sacrifice, determination, and faith. The path is the way, and light is the goal, in the same way that someone who has "lost their way" or "gone astray" veers onto the path of destruction. There is even a path metaphor amid the

vocabulary of war that has entered into colloquial use.
To be "on the warpath" implies that one is in rebellion,
has a hostile mindset, and is on the road to ruin.

✦

Two roads diverged in a yellow wood,
And sorry I could not travel both
And be one traveler, long I stood
And looked down one as far as I could
To where it bent in the undergrowth;

Then took the other, as just as fair,
And having perhaps the better claim
Because it was grassy and wanted wear;
Though as for that the passing there
Had worn them really about the same,

And both that morning equally lay
In leaves no step had trodden black.
Oh, I kept the first for another day!
Yet knowing how way leads on to way,
I doubted if I should ever come back.

I shall be telling this with a sigh
Somewhere ages and ages hence:

Two roads diverged in a wood, and I—
I took the one less traveled by,
And that has made all the difference.

"The Road Not Taken" is one of the most well-known poems by American poet Robert Frost. The poem spoke to me the first time I read it, but I misunderstood its message. This happens to a lot of readers. The poem is often interpreted metaphorically, and I believe the reader does this unconsciously. It has been viewed as symbolic of what we both believe and wish to be the fundamental task in our lives, that of choosing the right path, which is always the narrower one. The poem touched a nerve when it was published in 1916 and it continues to do so today. Many readers interpret it to be about making a choice to choose "the road less traveled," to go their own way, and thus to stay true to themselves. Such a message fits perfectly into commencement speeches to young people who are on the cusp of adulthood.

Since this is how "The Road Not Taken" is most often understood, it's somewhat ironic that Robert Frost did not have this meaning in mind when he wrote the poem.

The poem consists of four stanzas, but it is the last three lines that are most frequently quoted:

Two roads diverged in a wood, and I—
I took the one less traveled by,
And that has made all the difference.

Robert Faggen, a professor of literature who has analyzed the poem, does not see it as an expression of free will. On the contrary, Faggen believes it is an expression of determinism. If I understand Faggen's analysis correctly, it is not the narrator's freedom of choice that causes him to doubt which path he should choose. The poem's narrator in fact has no freedom of choice. He is born to doubt; doubt is his most basic characteristic. The story goes that Robert Frost first composed the poem as a joke for the poet Edward Thomas, who always struggled in making decisions. As with most of the poem's readers, Thomas never grasped the poem's irony and took it to be an insult from his friend.

Robert Frost's biographer, Lawrance Thompson, writes that the poem's narrator is a person who habitually wastes his energy because he regrets all the things he has decided for and sighs over those he's decided against. He also claims that during readings, Frost would often say the poem's narrator was based on his friend Edward Thomas, who in Frost's own words, was a person who "No matter which road he took, he always wished he'd taken another."

✦

THE NORDMARKA WAS finally before us. We crossed the asphalt road and entered the forest, John ahead and me behind. We wanted to attempt to reach the mountain ridges to the west but we didn't have too many hours before daylight would begin to wane. We hoped that as long as we were walking at an incline, we would also be heading west, and that once we reached the top of our chosen ridge, the view would allow us to look deeper in toward the forest. From there, we might even have enough of a perspective to choose our course going forward. It was impossible to judge how long it might take us to get to the ridge top. The going went more slowly than I had expected, and it was much harder.

THE PATH IS order in chaos. Its significance is revealed only after you have walked through a forest without a path. If the forest is large, the possibilities are endless. You can choose any direction, but which way will you go, and what will you encounter?

The function of the path is not only to show you the way but also to reduce the number of decisions that must be made. For this reason, the path becomes much more valuable in a wooded setting than in any other landscape. The American travel writer Bill Bryson once decided to hike the Appalachian Trail, the 2,190-mile trail that runs from Georgia to Maine. At the time he hiked it, it was still considered the world's longest trail. In his book *A Walk in the Woods: Rediscovering America on the Appalachian Trail*, he describes the forest as a place unlike any other. The forest is three-dimensional. The trees crowd over and around you, blocking out every view.

If you look at a forest from a distance, it appears flat and dry and orderly like a garden, not unlike the green patch that marks it on a map. It's impossible to think it could be difficult to cross, but as soon as you enter the trees, you lose the overview.

The Nordmarka forest was neither flat nor dry nor orderly. It was dense, hilly, and wet. There were large boulders everywhere, fallen trees, slick roots covered with half-rotten leaves, a soft marshy ground that sapped our energy, and trees that dropped the last pieces of autumn over our heads as we walked.

We stopped every ten minutes. We turned around and retraced our steps. It was impossible to determine how long we had been walking, how quickly, or whether we were headed in the right direction. John mentioned the ancient custom of using anthills to orient oneself. I had also heard of this, so we decided to try it. There were anthills everywhere, but we soon realized that they were not always built against the south side of a tree, as we had been told. The anthills were constructed on every side of the trees: east, west, north, and south. As such, they were virtually useless as directional markers.

"You can't trust anything these days," John mumbled, "not even anthills." He kept walking.

We zigzagged up mountainsides. We zigzagged down ridges, meandering the way rivers do. It became more and more apparent that John was better at orientation than me. He not only had a better sense of direction, he was also better at paying attention. He took note of the terrain, paused to look around, tilted his head back, and gazed up at the sky. I, on the other hand, lost focus after only a short time. A thought would pop into my mind, and then another one, and another. I let my mind go off on tangents for ten minutes at a time without thinking about which direction we were headed, and then I would suddenly remember when John stopped up ahead of me and asked which way I thought we should go next.

A FEW DAYS earlier, I had met with Kenneth Buch, the coach for the Norwegian national orienteering team. I had called him up to ask if we could discuss the sport of orienteering, the physical exertion required by the runners, and even more importantly, the mental aspect. My theory was that the mental demands play a significant role in this sport, which Buch was able to confirm. Orienteering is extremely demanding mentally. The runners are required to make decisions at every turn, he said, and mentioned studies that show people who practice orienteering as children are better equipped to make independent choices as adults. As he spoke, I thought of Robert Frost's friend Edward Thomas, and how lucky it was for humanity that he chose poetry instead of orienteering in his youth. If he had chosen the latter, not only would he have been a terrible runner, but also the poem "The Road Not Taken" would never have been written.

The basic rules of orienteering are simple. The runner must find their way to particular locations, or control points, in the terrain by navigating with a compass and a topographical map on which the control points are marked. The goal is to locate the control points as quickly as possible and in a specific order. The runner may choose the starting direction.

Once the runner has decided on their route, they must then make decisions about several things: How should I reach the point as quickly as possible? How should I reach the point as simply as possible?

When the runner finds a control point, they stop and figure out how to get to the next point. The first thing to do is to check the map and make a decision about which direction and course to follow next. Then they are off running again, making many small decisions as they go, sometimes choosing detours that veer away from the path they chose at the previous point. The landscape sets the conditions, and forested terrain is never monotonous and predictable. The ground varies; the view is limited; obstacles get in the way. The runner must always keep their gaze moving, from left to right, forward, down, up ahead as far as the eye can see.

Buch works with some of the best orienteers in the world. He explained to me that because orienteering ability improves with experience, runners are often at their peak around the age of thirty, which is older than athletes in many sports. To become a good orienteer, you first have to have a solid grasp of nature, he told me. You must know that certain trees grow only on solid ground, while others grow where the ground is soft. You must know where different animals tend to go and be able to follow their tracks, because animals think like us, or we think like them, and it is important to find the path of least resistance.

I told him about my forthcoming hike with John and asked if he had any tips for us. Without hesitation, he said, "The Nordmarka is a dense forest, which means it can be challenging to get an overview. Try to get up high whenever possible. It's easier to make good decisions and choose a route from up high. And, of course, be sure to follow the sun."

KENNETH BUCH'S WORDS buzzed in my head as I clawed my way up ridge after ridge. We were following his advice. We sought out high points as much as we were able, but we never saw the sun. The sky was gray and there were no visible bright spots among the clouds.

It began to get dark. It started to rain. The forest grew dim. Ice-cold drops fell from the sky. We reached the top of a large mountain range, but was this the range we had selected on our map?

I began to have the sneaking suspicion that it wasn't the same mountain range. I asked John what he thought. He looked around in all four directions but didn't respond. I asked him again: "Do you think we are on the right mountain range?" "No," John said, "I don't think so." With that, one of the most important principles of map navigation became clear to me.

It's one thing to start from a known point and navigate toward the next point from there. But if you have ended up somewhere and you don't know where that is, and you are supposed to walk toward a third point that is located somewhere that is also unclear, what you are is lost. You have made a number of small decisions, perhaps going a tiny bit farther astray each time, and in the end you are located in a state of total confusion and uncertainty. It's not unlike a consequential error in mathematics. It doesn't matter that you apply the formula correctly toward the end of the math problem if you have made a mistake at the beginning.

This was the situation in which we found ourselves. We didn't have the foggiest idea where we were; we guessed we might have taken a wrong turn in only the first few miles. Now we were on a mountain range we did not recognize or relate to. There were no paths here, no signs of civilization. There was also no view beyond fir trees as far as the eye could see. There was nothing but a vast green blanket that didn't reveal anything, not even vertical gradations.

The rain picked up. It was almost completely dark. John suggested we set up camp right where we were and hope for better luck with the weather the next day. Once the words were out of his mouth, it became obvious that this was the right thing to do. All we would accomplish by pushing on would be to get colder, wetter, and farther off-track.

We set up our tents in this arbitrary spot in the forest. No one knew where we were; even we didn't know.

It was possible no other humans had ever set foot here before because there had never been a reason to do so.

We set up our tents with the doors face to face. Each of us crawled into his tent, wriggling off our wet clothes and creeping into our sleeping bags. Before I fell asleep, I thought about paths and about the American philosopher and writer Henry David Thoreau who wrote in *Walden*: "A man needs only to be turned round once with his eyes shut in this world to be lost."

✛

I WOKE UP in my tent and pulled down the zipper. The sky outside was blue. The morning sun was warm. Steam rose from the heather; there was no wind. A thin ribbon of smoke rose white and silent in the morning light. John had already lit a fire and prepared coffee. I pulled on my wet clothes and went out. "Here," John said, handing me a cup. He wasn't only our guide on this expedition. He was also the expedition cook.

We ate breakfast, drank coffee, and let the fire burn out. Then we packed our gear and turned to the impossible task of planning our course. We knew that the sun was now located in the east. This helped us to determine which direction was south. But what we still didn't know was how deep into the forest we had come.

Were we parallel with Oslo so that we should turn and head south? Should we continue heading west, or had we already walked too far in that direction? We settled on something in the middle and began to walk in the direction we believed was southwest. John once again walked ahead and I walked behind. The forest shut like a zipper behind us, as thick and silent as the earth itself.

I HAVE WALKED on many paths, from Australia in the southern hemisphere to Iceland in the north. Through cultural landscapes. Through the wilderness. Over scorching steppes. Through damp rain forests. To the top of volcanoes. I have walked in impenetrable mangrove forests. Across the tundra-like moraine ridges of the high mountains. Through green, undulating plains with grass that reached to my shoulders. I have walked through stony wastelands so barren and bleak, so naked to the bone and desolate that it was like walking across the earth before everything began, or after everything was over.

Walking in the rain forest was like walking through a cathedral. Everything was quiet, cool, and dusky: a sacral ambience beneath vaults of green like a church roof. I walked at the foot of the trees, across fallen leaves the size of dinner plates. I felt as small as a hobbit and never, before or since, have I ever felt so happy to be on a path. The path was my salvation. I knew if I were to lose it, I would be swallowed up by the forest, entirely lost.

Walking through the mangrove forests was even worse, if that's possible. The mangroves are as old as time itself and among the most hardy and steadfast living beings on the earth. Mangroves and cockroaches: in the future, they may be the only two forms of life to remain on the planet.

I had wanted to walk from one beach to another. The mangrove forest was so small that I could see the other beach from where I stood. A small path led through the forest, but the path followed an arc and I wanted to get to the second beach quickly so I began to walk in a straight line. After thirty feet I regretted that decision. Dense forests were nothing new to me, but the trees I was used to were submissive, with branches you could push to the side if the growth got too thick. The mangroves were different. They were stiff and hard, immovable as iron. By the time I reached the other side of the forest, I was overheated. My shorts and new khaki-colored shirt, designed specifically for tropical climates, were both shredded. My legs and arms were covered with scratches. I looked like the nineteenth-century explorer David Livingstone must have on his journeys into central Africa, and I knew with absolute certainty that I would never again cross a mangrove forest unless there was a wide and clearly marked trail running through it.

THE TREES IN the Nordmarka forest are more pliable than mangroves. The forest is more open than a rain forest, but it was dense enough for John and me. We chanced across a high point affording a view over the surrounding landscape, but it didn't help much because the view was limited and as soon as we were down among the trees again, we couldn't see anything.

We continued to run into new hills and ridges, hindrances we had to surmount, swamps we had to circumvent. There was no way of knowing our speed or how far we had already walked. We picked blueberries and drank water from icy creeks. Single beams of light pushed through the trees so that the shadows from our bodies and from the trees pointed us in the direction we should walk. Or was it so late in the day now that the shadows were pointing north instead? We couldn't know with any certainty, and we were not allowed to check the time—that was one of the strictest rules of the expedition.

The forest floor was saturated with moisture. Ancient deciduous trees lay strewn helter-skelter. Chanterelle mushrooms that no one had spotted gleamed like tiny fires under the trees. Green and yellow, brown and gray: these were the only colors among the undergrowth. We spotted animal tracks everywhere; they had formed paths along the streams. There was no sound besides the water gurgling and our own heavy breathing.

I tripped over an old skull, white and brittle, half-way covered in green moss. The eyeholes were dark and empty. The molars were flat and there were no sharp canine teeth. There was something melancholy and pure about the scene, and I stopped and looked at it for a long time. A moose calf had once ended its days in this very spot, a moose calf that would come to occupy my thoughts for many months after our hike.

We struggled on through the forest. Crows cawed at regular intervals in the crowns of trees overhead. I sometimes caught a glimpse of them, black as ink, as disturbing as messengers from the afterlife. It wasn't hard to understand why crows sit in treetops. From that vantage point, they have the overview that is lacking at ground level. The crows were able to see everything. John and I could see nothing. The forest was not a problem for them, and if we could speak their language, I would have politely asked them for directions.

Humans have always thought of birds as guides. Explorers used birds' terrestrial routes to find the way to uncharted territories. They knew the birds migrated and understood that if they were to follow them, they would sooner or later reach land. The Polynesians studied the migratory patterns of birds for several years before following them. The Vikings did it too. In the Biblical story of Noah's ark, birds are the first sign that the mainland has reappeared after the great flood. Noah sends a dove to see whether the waters have receded, and the dove returns with an olive branch in its beak.

I WAS BROUGHT up to believe that if I get lost in a large forest, I will sooner or later end up where I started. Without knowing it, people who are lost will always walk in a circle. In the book *Finding Your Way Without Map or Compass*, author Harold Gatty confirms that this is true. We walk in circles for several reasons. The most important is that virtually no human has two legs of the exact same length. One leg is always slightly longer than the other, and this causes us to turn without even noticing it. In addition, everyone has a dominant eye, and if you are hiking with a backpack on, the weight of that backpack will inevitably throw you off balance. Our dominant hand factors into the mix too. If you are right-handed, you will have a tendency to turn toward the right. And when you meet an obstacle, you will subconsciously decide to pass it on the right side. Similarly, if it is windy and raining and the wind is blowing at you from the side, you will turn your face away from it so the rain hits your back. In doing so, without noticing it you will veer away from the rain and into the opposite direction.

I thought about this idea as we walked. The sun was shining and there was no wind, but both John and I are right-handed. Maybe, without even knowing it, we had been turning slightly in that direction ever since the start of our hike?

A SENSE OF direction and the ability to orient oneself and to judge distances were all vital skills for humans of the Stone Age. Such skills are hardly needed today, and maybe because of this we've started to lose them. They've been relegated to the dustiest corners of the human brain, eventually to become as useless as armpit hair or male nipples.

Not long ago, I was in Iceland with friends of mine to do some fly-fishing. We rented a car at the airport and drove around the gorgeous island. A week later, I was responsible for directing us back to the airport and I typed in the desired location and looked at the GPS. A soft, calm female voice told us everything we needed to know.

"In two miles, you will come to a roundabout."

"Take the second exit."

"The next turn is in six kilometers."

"Turn left."

"Turn right."

Outside the car windows, one of the most beautiful and unique landscapes in the world flashed by but I didn't see it. I was staring at the screen as though the entire trip were taking place on an animated landscape and I was a participant on a TV game show, not a traveler on the saga island of Iceland.

A few days later, while listening to the news on the radio, I heard the announcer refer to a story that had just taken place. According to the report, three friends in Vermont, out for a drive in a borrowed car during rain and heavy fog, had a rather unfortunate experience. Their GPS led them out onto an ice-covered lake, after which the ice broke under the weight of the car and sank. The friends were able to escape the sinking car, which was not retrieved until a week later. Google, which owns the GPS software, had no explanation for what happened.

"It is a surprising and memorable, as well as valuable experience, to be lost in the woods any time," writes Henry David Thoreau in Walden. *In her book* A Field Guide to Getting Lost, *Rebecca Solnit cites the German philosopher Walter Benjamin: "To be lost is to be fully present."*

We are guilty not only of trusting the GPS navigational capabilities of our smartphones; we also believe that they will save us if we get lost. As long as we have our phones with us, we consider ourselves safe. This is why what was completely commonplace only a few decades ago—namely, going to the mountains without any possibility of contacting others—is now considered an act of insanity. In fact, our smartphones provide a false sense of security that it is no longer possible to get lost, even though it is. A GPS is less reliable than a map, your own navigational skills, and your ability to read the landscape and to follow along as you walk.

The great explorers always got lost. Traveling to places no one had ever been before, and therefore never being certain where they were, was the basic assumption of such a journey. Even if they had principally gotten lost, the explorers would never have thought about their situation in such terms. It was a desired condition, just like it was for the Stone Age humans as they followed the edge of the ice north.

When do you know with certainty that you are lost? When the world has become so large that you no longer recognize it. Solnit tells of the Wintu Tribe from northern California. The Wintu language does not use the terms "right" or "left" to describe directions; instead, it refers to the cardinal directions: north, south, east, west. The Wintu "I," the pronoun that mediates understanding of oneself in the world, does not exist in isolation but rather in relation to the surrounding landscape. There is no "you" without mountains, without sun, without sky, writes Solnit.

THE HOURS PASSED quickly in the Nordmarka forest. We adjusted our course along with the shifting sun. If it were summertime, the sun would be directly overhead at noon. But where was it now, in October, when its path across the sky was lower and shorter?

We had no idea where we were. The landscape all looked the same; there was nothing on either side but dense forest and silence. All around us were these spaces beneath the trees that no one has ever seen— shy places without humans where only plants sprout up, grow, wither, and die; where rain falls; where animals pass, soundless. Here in these spaces where there are no voices, one must ask that old philosophical question: If a tree falls in the forest and no one hears it, has it, in fact, made a sound?

We passed a hilltop that seemed higher than the others. We were on our way down a dark ravine with a small stream at its base when we noticed the tops of the trees to our left. John suggested we climb up to see whether we might have a better view from above. I was exhausted. I was tired of walking off-trail. I no longer believed that the hilltops or ridges would afford us a good view. It was not a tempting prospect to deliberately go uphill, but I knew John had a good point, so we clambered up to the top, and from there we were rewarded with the best view so far.

The sun was on its way down in the west. In the same direction, we saw the top of a hill that appeared higher than the rest. It basked in the soft evening sunlight, like a sleeping dinosaur in the middle of the endless forest. Between us and it was a deep, wide valley covered with fir trees. There was no way of knowing how long it would take us to get to the other side of the valley and up the hill. It might be one mile or it might be five.

To our south was a body of water. It twinkled alluringly in the low evening sun and we decided to head in that direction. We followed the small stream and continued down the steep ravine. We were walking downhill and we finally knew where to go. It wouldn't be long now. Soon we would pitch our tents, put on dry clothes, and sit on a couple of rocks eating a big dinner next to a crackling fire.

At the base of the ravine, the terrain flattened out. We thrashed our way through a thick area of underbrush and emerged into a clearing. An old cabin with dark, untreated log walls and a rusty corrugated roof was situated there. A sign on the door showed a blue emblem with a white bear against a brown background. Beneath the emblem were the words:

Encampment for the Milgor platoon 100/13001 during training 1941–45.

The cabin and the sign were reminders that the Nordmarka forest had been one of the most important hiding places for the Norwegian resistance movement during the war. This is where they would meet, in a log cabin in a clearing in the middle of a great forest; this is where they would hide and plan acts of sabotage. In a place to which no paths led because the resisters did not wish to be discovered.

SOME MINUTES LATER, the water from the surface of the lake gleamed through the trees. Our mood picked up. We whooped and laughed. We strolled along the edge of the water until we found a west-facing promontory with warm, smooth stones. We put up our tents. We lay out our wet clothes to dry on the bank. We took out our food and gathered wood and, when darkness descended, we lit a big fire and dug our watches, maps, phones, and the GPS from the bottom of the backpack.

The information was shocking.

The blue line that showed up on the phone's map displayed the route we had taken. It wound its way through the terrain like the electronic graph of a heart patient who is about to die. It led in constant zigzags, never for a single stretch following a straight line. On the first day, we had walked four-and-a-half miles. On the second day, we walked nine miles. We had walked for fourteen hours but we had covered no more than thirteen-and-a-half miles all together. Our average speed was less than one mile per hour, which is almost four times slower than if we had been walking on a path.

When measured in a straight line, our journey had taken us just three-and-a-half miles from the train station where we first set off. Our goal to walk in a straight line had been a complete and utter failure. We had walked four times as far as we would have if we had followed a straight line. That meant that for every one step we took forward, we had taken practically four steps to the side. We had danced our way through the forest. One step forward, four to the left. One step forward, four to the right.

We sat next to the fire and looked out at the landscape around us. The final inklings of light were beginning to fade. The sky was a pale red, almost pink where the sun had dipped behind the trees. Higher up it was deep blue and as transparent as newly formed ice. The water was a mirror. The trees shimmered red and yellow. The first stars began to show themselves. Then the colors vanished. Within a moment they were gone, as if an invisible force had sucked them into the earth.

THE NEXT MORNING, we packed our bags and followed paths back to Oslo, and in the following weeks I thought about this peculiar experience of ours. The memories would surface at random, while I was out shopping for groceries, sitting in the office writing, or just as I was dropping off to sleep. I thought about the feeling of getting lost, of finding yourself on the forest floor beneath the old trees in absolute silence; I thought about the dim light, the animal tracks, and the skull from that poor moose calf. I thought about that skull constantly. It became the image for me of wild and untouched nature, this moose that was born and then died without anyone noticing—somewhere in the vast forest, outside of any path, outside of the world, or perhaps precisely within it, the way it is meant to be.

PART
III

TRACKS

BEFORE THERE IS a path, there are tracks. A path is created only after multiple footprints and tracks have been trodden in the same place, because a path is the result of organized movement. But what about all the tracks made by animals that don't follow paths, those that simply amble around without a particular plan, acting on basic impulses or searching for food in some location they don't quite know?

Some among us are still skilled at finding and reading animal tracks. Hunters and nature photographers are able to pick out animal tracks that the average hiker would never see. And not only can they detect tracks that are nearly invisible to the rest of us, they are also able to discern which animal created them, when the tracks were made, and what direction the animal was heading. Throughout the generations, indigenous peoples have developed their ability to read the tracks in nature. Stone Age peoples must have mastered these skills.

As a child, I enjoyed reading books and comics about the indigenous peoples of North America. They were all good trackers. But what about those of us with little to no experience in interpreting and following tracks? Believe it or not, we still have the chance to try our hand at track tracing, at least those of us living in subarctic regions. Such an opportunity, however, is completely dependent on the weather.

TWO MONTHS HAD passed since John and I returned from our off-trail hike through the Nordmarka. We had spoken on the phone several times since then about how strange the experience had been, about how the forest had revealed a totally different side than we were used to seeing. John said he had been reading anything he could get his hands on about navigation and orienteering. He wanted us to undertake several more such explorations, and I agreed wholeheartedly.

It's a steep learning curve when you practice new skills rather than just reading about them. You make one mistake after another, but the second time you try a slightly different way and slowly you start to develop an understanding of how things work. John and I agreed we were better at finding trails now than before we went on our expedition. At the same time, we also both agreed that we had a whole lot to learn before we could ever hold a candle to the indigenous peoples depicted in the cartoons we used to watch in the 1970s. We decided to plan a new trip for the following summer. But first we would have to get through the long, cold winter.

CHRISTMAS APPROACHED. THE thermometer dropped below freezing for the first time, and I went walking and waited for the snow. Nothing is better than freshly fallen snow if one is hoping to document movement. Even the tiniest creatures leave behind clear tracks on a soft snow layer, and my plan was to follow the tracks to gain insight into what the animals that made them must have been thinking, how they had moved, and where they were headed.

When the first big snowfall finally came, I dropped everything and went straight to the forest. It was a sunny Sunday afternoon. It had already snowed the day before, large white flakes over the city. Toward evening, the clouds disappeared. It stopped snowing. The temperature rose and the snow turned soft and slushy. I followed the weather forecast like an air traffic controller, checking my phone every five minutes to note any meteorological changes. By the time I went to bed late that night it was still above freezing, but when I awoke at dawn the next day I was happy to see that the temperature had dipped below freezing again. Everything was exactly as I'd hoped. The snow had been sufficiently wet during the night to allow the animals' footprints to sink down into it. This, I theorized, should mean that the early morning freeze had solidified those tracks like plaster casts.

I rode the subway toward the same stretch of forest that John and I had traversed two months earlier.

A parking lot bordered the edge of the forest. By the time I arrived, it was already half full of cars with skis on their roof racks and people in tracksuits talking loudly and jovially to each other. The grooming machine had already laid down parallel sets of tracks, and the skiers were happy to start the season. Cross-country, or Nordic, skiing is so closely linked with Norwegian identity that we tend to view this moment—the first ski trip of the year—as one of the most important of our lives. It is the occasion on which we feel we are living most in harmony with ourselves and our heritage.

I crossed the parking lot and disappeared in between the trees, away from the groomed ski tracks. The sounds of cheerful laughter and newly waxed skis gliding over dry powder continued to reach my ears for a long time, until they finally became fainter and fainter and then it was silent. The snow had covered every surface. The landscape, which throughout the fall months had slowly turned brown and bare, a composted reality apparently devoid of any life, suddenly appeared pristine and shiny new again.

Few things make Norwegians happier than cross-country skiing on a brisk, sunny Sunday in winter. We seize the opportunity, and it's not all that hard to understand why, because ski tracks are a temporary path. They are laid down in December and vanish by April, and there are some winters when too little snow falls and they aren't even laid down at all.

Cross-country, or Nordic, ski tracks are tracks made by a machine. Some trail systems provide two sets of parallel tracks, offering skiers the opportunity to pass each other, to ski side by side, or to stop for a little break. In Norway, the tracks often lead to heated shelters that serve simple meals, and the trail networks are clearly marked with signs that inform you where you are going, how long you still have to go, and how long it will take to return if you decide to turn around.

Most skiers stick to the groomed trails, but if you follow the machine-made tracks through the woods, every now and then you will notice a set of rough ski tracks that slips away through the trees. These are the tracks of skiers who have chosen to follow their own path—driven perhaps by the urge to explore, social anxiety, rebellion against conformity, or any variety of other reasons. The only traces left by these lone skiers are two lines in the snow and a series of small holes on either side where their pole tips have hit.

I was that kind of skier on this beautiful winter morning. I wanted to make my own path. I hoped to discover what and who and how many had been padding through this forest since the previous night's snowfall. Would there be a lot of tracks? Would there be none? I harbored no assumptions about what I might see.

RESEARCHERS HAVE LONG believed that the first life-forms crawled up onto land two hundred to three hundred million years ago. Not long ago, however, in an alpine area in southeast Poland, a 397-million-year-old track made by a tetrapod, a four-legged vertebrate that adapted to life on land, was discovered.

Archeologists in Kenya have found tracks dating back a million and a half years, footprints showing bipedal movement that apparently originated with one of our own ancestors, *Homo erectus*.

Ancient tracks from bipedal creatures have also been found in Europe. The oldest, discovered in Norfolk,

England, are believed to be close to one million years old. These tracks also come from one of our ancestors, *Homo antecessor*.

It doesn't stop there. On the Greek island of Crete, archeologists uncovered humanlike tracks that may be as old as 5.7 million years old, put down by *Australopithecus*, another of our distant relatives.

I'M NO ARCHEOLOGIST. It was not ancient traces I was looking for in the forest that December morning. I was on a hunt for something new: fresh tracks made in the night by creatures that were still close by.

I thought I might have to go looking for them, but the tracks soon proved to be everywhere. An incredible number of animals had passed this way, even though the snow had fallen only hours ago and the forest touched up right to the edge of the city. The signs of all the previous night's events were clearly written before me, yet I would never have made this discovery if not for the snow. I saw the sharp outlines of roe deer tracks, the larger ones left by moose, the soft ones of the fox. The tracks of the rabbits were unmistakable. They are the first tracks children learn to recognize in science class: two small paws in front and two behind, the first two behind each other, the last two beside each other. It is the kind of track left by an animal that hops.

Beneath the pine trees, the squirrel had left its characteristic track, a trail of cones sprinkled across the snow like cinnamon on rice pudding. I saw tracks from mice and other small rodents. Some of them were no more than a quarter of an inch wide, and these had clear claw marks. I saw the tracks of birds that had flitted about on the snow and the marks from their wings that had brushed the snow aside when they lifted off.

Some tracks went in straight lines. Others wound in arcs or zigzags across the forest floor. Sometimes the animals had stopped to change direction. Suddenly they had veered ninety degrees to the right, continued for a few yards, and then turned ninety degrees to the left, tracing a slight curve back to the right again. At other times, they had walked in circles or turned and headed back the way they had come. I pictured them, sticking their little and big snouts into the snow, lifting their heads, looking around, listening and sensing the air, and then continuing on. Some of them had most likely been born in the spring or early summer and were thus experiencing snow for the very first time.

I was apparently the first human in this part of the forest after the previous night's snowfall. It was a situation I found both pleasant and unpleasant. Being the first person to lay down tracks made me feel like an explorer, but also left me feeling exposed. If someone should happen by, they couldn't fail to notice my ski tracks, which would be easy enough to follow. In the books and comics I had read as a child, the indigenous peoples had a trick to confuse their pursuers: they would walk. Then they would stop and walk backward in their own tracks so those following them would think they had vanished into thin air.

I ventured deeper into the forest, captivated by all the tracks and the miniscule stories about secret lives in places unknown to humans. Time passed. The afternoon approached, and when I finally decided to return to the parking lot I realized I no longer knew where I was. There was no one else around, no one to ask, no sign telling me where I was. The usual hiking paths were buried under the snow and therefore useless, but it wasn't hard to find my way back. All I had to do was to turn around and retrace my own ski tracks.

+

THAT SAME NIGHT, it snowed even more—two feet of fresh snow—and the next morning I took the opportunity to investigate. This time, instead of heading to the forest, I stayed in the city. It was only seven o'clock and, as those who live far north in the northern hemisphere know, this meant it would still be dark for several hours.

I left early in order to study the walking habits of people on their way to work: busy businesspeople with hand-sewn dress shoes and more important jobs than mine. I assumed most of them would be in a hurry, which might allow me to read some interesting facts into their rushed morning movements. This time I was neither a pathfinder nor an archeologist, I was a social anthropologist. What I hoped to study was the human inclination to choose shortcuts, alternative paths that would be easy enough to document in the freshly fallen snow.

Why do we so often break with the pattern of movement that landscape architects and city planners want us to take? They put up fences and hedges, put down gravel on the paths, and erect signs, but to no avail. People will always choose where they want to walk. We take shortcuts across areas where landscape planners don't want us to walk; it is a quiet form of rebellion against uniformity and conformity.

I watched the pedestrian commuters in the morning rush and the tracks they left behind in the snow. The expression "to go one's own way" was no longer just a metaphor; it became concrete and real, like a new dimension being uncovered layer by layer. Human movement patterns: sometimes they resulted from conscious choices, but more often they came from unconscious ones. Which way will I choose and why, which way, which way?

In his book *On Trails: An Exploration*, author Robert Moor writes about a professor of urban planning at the University of Stuttgart who in the 1980s began study- ing the well-worn footpaths on the campus grounds where he worked. Across all the university green spaces were shortcuts that ran between the paved walkways. The professor conducted an experiment in which he hid these shortcuts by planting new grass over them, and as he suspected, new paths were soon worn into the same places where the older ones had been.

I had noticed the same thing. There is a university not far from where I live, and I often go there to check out books from the library. On the way, I cross over the university lawns, the same ones I crossed when I was a student. The grass is crisscrossed with shortcuts that students walk over and over again, two by two, or three in a row, chattering on their way to lectures.

HUMANS WILL ALWAYS choose shortcuts if we can and if we believe it's beneficial to us. We unconsciously and instinctively evaluate the situation: How much time will I save by choosing the shortcut over the path the city planners and landscape architects have dreamed up? Our brains make decisions based on a simple formula: time on one side of the equation and energy on the other. If the energy required is less than the time we will save, we choose the shortcut. If the opposite is true, we follow the route laid out by the city planners.

This approach is most apparent in city and residential environments. If two paved walkways intersect at a forty-five-degree angle with a patch of lawn between them, people will inevitably cut a path across the lawn because it saves time and because walking across a patch of lawn requires no energy. In such situations, people will always cut corners, and those whose job it is to draw and design our cities and towns must factor in this behavior whenever they start a new project.

"Walkability" is an important term in modern city planning. It describes a method for measuring how pedestrian-friendly an area is, and it includes parameters such as the surroundings, the presence or absence of paths or sidewalks, the amount of vehicle traffic, the degree of safety for pedestrians, and the general condition of sidewalks and trails.

City planners should shape the built environment in such a way that people follow the intended pedestrian routes. But people will always choose their own paths. They will protest if faced with unreasonable restrictions. It's impossible to tame us—any dictator or kindergarten teacher knows this—and this fact was emphatically confirmed to me during this winter morning rush hour. By eight o'clock, almost every single corner I observed had been bisected. Small grooved paths had been trodden into the snow, compressed by busy people wearing expensive dress shoes on their way to work.

MENTAL
DETOURS

HAT WINTER WAS the coldest and longest in many years. January began with temperatures of minus four degrees Fahrenheit and near-complete darkness. February came, then March. The sidewalks were slick as soap. The children were in heaven. Elderly people slipped and fell and went to the hospital with broken hips. Within the forest, the snow was piled four to five feet deep. I had tired of cross-country skiing; I wanted to be able to go for walks again, but it was impossible to walk anywhere. It wasn't until the end of March that the sun's warmth was strong enough for the new season to break through.

Then the snow slowly began to melt on the roads, but the forest paths stayed buried under two feet of dirty snow. I was tired of sitting still, so early one morning I decided to walk out of the city on a backroad I knew about. The road crossed fields and passed farms, wound around a lake and along a wooded area, and I decided I would walk until I had gone six-and-a-half miles. Then I would turn around and walk home again, and in this way I would end up walking thirteen miles, roughly the equivalent of a half-marathon. The plan this time was to walk as fast as I could. It was my first real walk in three months, and I wanted to start the season with a bang.

I don't enjoy running. I've tried establishing a habit of telling my body that running is just a natural part of existing. It has worked at times. I've pushed myself to go running for a couple of months, but I always know the habit won't last, the way a devoted smoker who decides to quit smoking without much conviction knows it won't be long before they take up that habit again.

Walking always gives me the sense that I have enough time, that I'm not in a rush. There's no reason to get stressed out because there is a maximum speed at which a person can walk. Regardless of how rapidly one walks, it will always be at a much slower pace than someone who is running or driving a car. Walkers get used to this. They learn to value the slow pace of walking. They reach their destination on time because they become accustomed to how long it will take to get there on foot.

One of the many stories told about the philosopher Arne Næss is an interview he once gave. Næss was a passionate mountain climber and the interview was about climbing.

The journalist asked, "Why did you start climbing?"

Næss replied, "Why did you stop?"

The same could be said about walking. Walking is a necessary part of life, an ordinary act of moving the body from one place to another—to take out the trash, stand by the stove, go down the stairs or up the stairs, walk along a path or over to visit the neighbor—and back again.

Since walking is such a normal part of our daily life, we don't consider it a sport like running. When you walk, you don't need spandex pants or a headband or one of those strange upper-arm configurations that joggers often wear as if it were a defibrillator or pepper spray and they were running through Baltimore's most dangerous alleyways.

I walk on forest paths. I walk on city sidewalks. I walk on country roads.

Walking on a path is an adventure. No step is ever the same as another. One never knows what might be waiting around the next bend. The terrain varies, the ground cover varies, and the body must exert itself in a number of ways. As exercise, walking on paths is the best. I've heard stories about people who have walked their way out of spinal prolapses and depression after doctors and psychologists have tried for years to help them.

The best thing about walking in the city is that it doesn't attract any attention. You are simply a person walking among other people. No one notices you, no one knows where you're going, how far you've come, or for how long you plan to continue. Walking in the city is an activity you can do without interruption and that, together with the rhythm it creates in the body and head, is most likely the reason that so many thinking people have used walking as a means to achieve higher goals. Friedrich Nietzsche. Charles Darwin. Søren Kierkegaard. Virginia Woolf. They all walked, even if some of them used different or more illustrious words for the activity.

There are, namely, many different types of walking.

To walk is the practical variant. We walk from one place to another because we have something we need to do, and the act of walking is a means of getting there. A walker is not thinking about important things, but rather allows their thoughts to meander.

To saunter is the low-threshold variation of walking. A saunterer walks slowly. They do not have any particular goal in mind with their sauntering, and they rarely go far. Someone who saunters is thinking small, practical thoughts, often with hands clasped behind their back. Older people tend to saunter.

To stroll is a distinctly bourgeois form of walking undertaken by those with a keen awareness of class differences. Whoever takes a stroll most often enjoys doing it with others while discussing politics and other topics of societal significance. Strolling has nothing to do with paths; it usually takes place in urban settings and frequently ends with a visit to a café.

To hike, or *to wander* as is the Germanic word for hiking, is a form that differs from walking in three important ways. First, hiking implies expectations about a particular distance and, as such, one doesn't hike over to the neighbor's house to borrow some sugar. Second, hiking implies thinking important thoughts and taking in the landscape's aesthetic qualities while underway. Third, hiking takes place almost exclusively on trails or paths. Romantic poets of the 1880s were often referred to as "wandering poets" because of their penchant for long hikes on trails while they pondered the world around them. Such poets often emphasized the experience of the sublime in nature through their writing.

THE DEFINITION OF walking is having one foot on the ground at any given time. The definition of running is having both feet located in midair between each step.

There's something extraordinarily sustainable about walking. It's difficult to imagine that it harms anyone, and under normal circumstances it can be carried out in every conceivable manner from the time we are around a year old until we die, or at least until right before we die. In other words, to become someone who loves walking is a long-term investment for which you will receive returns every day of your life. Walking is the only form of exercise that does not require you to actively decide to exercise but that is rather merely an extension of the life you are already living and the activities you are already doing every day. If you want to transform your walking into exercise, all you have to do is walk a bit more often and a little farther than you usually do.

If I am able to leave the house early in the morning, I like to take more circuitous routes to the office so that my way there and back again in the evening are about five miles total. If I add another walk to my day, I end up walking a total distance of between thirty and forty miles per week. That adds up to a lot of miles each year without much exertion.

If I walk rapidly, I can walk four miles an hour. That means it takes me three hours to walk a half-marathon and six hours for a marathon without the experience being unpleasant. For me, unpleasantness is really what keeps me from running. The aching in my body, the stiffness in my muscles, the gasping for breath whenever I don't get enough oxygen, the pain in my knees suffering under my body's weight, the lack of distraction from the pain are just a start. I don't see anything when I run, I don't have any good ideas, and I don't solve any big problems. I can hardly think about anything other than my own exhausted body and when I can finally stop running.

WALKING ON A country road in our modern times is more problematic than hiking on paths through the forest or on sidewalks in the city. The French philosopher Jean-Jacques Rousseau loved to amble along country roads, but he lived in the 1700s when you were able to do such things without attracting attention. Nowadays, the act of walking along a country road is held to be completely devoid of sense and purpose. If you are found walking along a country road, people get suspicious. What's wrong with that person, they'll think. Why aren't they driving a car? Why aren't they taking the bus? What are they doing along the shoulder? Are they sick? Insane? On the run? Did they bury some loot and now they're returning to dig it up?

IT WAS EARLY morning when I began my half-marathon. I had decided to walk as rapidly as I possibly could. I walked through the neighborhoods of villas on the outskirts of the city and was soon on the country road. I walked six-and-a-half miles and then turned and walked back again. Six buses passed me along the way, as well as tractors, bicycles, and large logging trucks hauling the winter logs out of the forest. I met a jogger, an old man wearing a yellow reflective vest who was running as fast as he could, airing out his mortal dread as the author Dag Solstad once wrote, but he ran so slowly, his body stooped forward as if he were climbing a steep hill or advancing against hurricane-strength winds. It was a windless spring day and I walked faster than the old man was able to run.

A woman zoomed by in her Porsche Cayenne. She was on her way into the city. She wore enormous sunglasses and talked on her smartphone while she drove. When she noticed me, a person on foot along the narrow country road, she veered around me while turning her head to gawk. She downshifted and vanished over the ridge and the road was once again silent. The woman in the Porsche had vanished. The man with the reflective vest had vanished. I heard my own footsteps land on the asphalt and kick off again. I heard birdsong from the naked trees

along the road, and spotted moose and fox tracks in the
rotten snow in the fields.

FOR FRIEDRICH NIETZSCHE, Charles Darwin, Søren
Kierkegaard, and Virginia Woolf, walking was an arena
for thinking, a catalyst for both intellectual insight and
aesthetic experiences. In his book *Sporten (The Sport)*,
sociologist and historian of ideas Rune Slagstad writes:

> *To go walking means here to move oneself by foot from
> one place to another without haste and without exter-
> nal force. Walking for the sake of walking does not
> mean one cannot have a goal, such as summiting a
> mountain, looking for a vantage point, etc. But reach-
> ing these goals only serves to achieve the single purpose:
> to bring fullness to the walk. Walking without seeking
> to achieve a goal is a modern phenomenon with roots
> in romanticism. It requires an openness for the experi-
> ential state of walking.*

Slagstad quotes "Jotunheimen," a travel article by
the writer and illustrator Emanuel Mohn, which was
printed by the Norwegian Travel Association in 1944:

> *Of course, one can always reach the endpoint if one
> simply sets off. But what fun is it only to rush to get*

home when there is so much of life to be seen? It's bet-
ter then, to sit oneself down and wonder at it all, just
as it is, and if one is skilled at drawing, he can draw.
When one tires of hopping and dancing, he reclines in
a sunny spot and gazes up at the blue sky, or else packs
a pipe and enjoys a smoke with long, full breaths.

For me, walking is not so much about thinking as it is about *not* thinking, or at least not about anything important or complicated. Walking is accompanied largely by simple, practical thoughts, elementary solutions— and quite often, whenever I'm not walking in cities or in dense urban areas, I like to talk aloud to myself.

IT'S NEVER BEEN my experience that things get more complicated when I walk. On the contrary, everything becomes simpler and clearer. Thoughts come and go; they wander, as we like to say. This is especially apparent if I listen to a podcast, which I do often if I'm walking in the city or on a country road but never when I am walking on paths in the forest. It doesn't matter how interesting or exciting the podcast is. If I am listening to it while walking, I will, at some point, lose the thread because my thoughts inevitably venture out on their own mental detours. I start thinking about something that makes me think about something else, and my brain will keep going like this until I am suddenly aware once again of the voice prattling on in my ear.

The podcast might be about murder and madness and swindles and politics, but even when the episode is at its most thrilling or significant point, my brain goes on autopilot and I start thinking about my dead grandfather's messy garage, or how long it will take to get Donald Trump impeached, or the fact that I've never used a chainsaw and that I may never get the chance now since I have epilepsy.

All of these thoughts have passed through my brain before I even register that I've lost the thread of the podcast and have to start it all over again.

Walking stimulates my brain like this. I can't tame it. When my smartphone rings and I answer it while sitting down, I will, without a doubt, stand up soon after and start pacing while speaking. It happens every time, even though I don't make a conscious decision to do so. I answer the phone and inevitably I stand up and start walking back and forth until the call is over, and I believe I do this because it's easier for me to keep the conversation going when I am moving. It seems to flow more easily than if I'm sitting down.

It is also much easier to think when you walk, and to solve problems. Maybe that's why, in the comic books,

Uncle Scrooge paces while pondering his business troubles. He walks in circles in his enormous penthouse office, hands folded behind his back, eventually walking so many circles that he wears a deep circular groove into the floor.

On May 5, 2009, two Norwegian mercenary soldiers, Joshua French and Tjostolv Moland, were arrested in the Democratic Republic of the Congo and accused of having murdered their Congolese chauffeur, Abedi Kasongo, in a wooded area outside of Kisangani. The pair was condemned for murder and imprisoned under the worst imaginable conditions. Four years later, in 2013, Tjostolv Moland took his own life in the cell he shared with his friend, and it wasn't until 2017 that Joshua French was released and sent back to Norway. French gave the first interview following his release on the Norwegian podcast "Two White Men." After Moland's death, French says he got sick and became so depressed he bordered on apathy. The only things he did were to sleep and walk. Every day he got up and walked back and forth in a corridor that was only fifty feet long. He did this all day long until he was returned to his cell again at four o'clock in the afternoon. "I walked thousands of miles in that corridor," Joshua French tells his interviewer.

MY HALF-MARATHON WENT as it always does. When I returned home, I checked the app on my smartphone. The app registers my distance, average speed, and route. It showed that I had maintained my intended tempo of four-and-a-half miles per hour for about six-and-a-half miles, until I turned around. On the way back, my pace slackened noticeably. It was also notably uneven. Four-and-a-half miles per hour, then only two miles an hour, five, three, one, four. My speed varied the whole way back, and I could think of no explanation other than it must have to do with my concentration and focus. I was not all that exhausted physically, but the farther I walked, the freer my brain became. It entered into the flow zone, just as my body did. It was no longer controlled; it took over my body and a stream of consciousness became my mental modus operandi. Every time my brain became engaged with something especially interesting, my pace slowed, and when it wasn't very engaged, my pace picked up again. When my brain worked harder, my body worked less. When my body worked more, my brain was working less. The only conclusion I can draw is this: a person who walks slowly must have a much richer inner life than a person who runs as fast as their legs can carry them.

There are three walkers in particular who fascinate me. Two of them are Americans, Edward Payson

Weston (1839–1929) and Emma Gatewood (1887–1973). The third is a Norwegian named Bjørn Amsrud.

Edward Payson Weston was an icon in his time. He was part of a movement that reached its zenith in the second half of the 1800s and that went by the name "pedestrianism," or walking as a sport. Pedestrianism was big in both Europe and the US, and it developed into an athletic activity with heavy competitive leanings and broad popular support. Weston was among the best pedestrians. In 1913, at the age of seventy-four, he walked from New York to Minneapolis, a distance of 1,546 miles in fifty-one days. His greatest strength was that he apparently required very little rest for rejuvenation. He could walk for hours at a time, sit down on a rock, eat a bite and drink a bit of water, and after that he was good as new.

EMMA GATEWOOD WAS sixty-seven years old when she packed her bag on May 3, 1955, and left Gallia County, Ohio, the only place she had ever lived. She hitchhiked to Charleston, West Virginia, flew to Atlanta, and took the bus to the little town of Jasper in Georgia. From there, she paid a taxi to take her to the foot of Mount Oglethorpe, where she began walking. When she got to the top, she found herself at the southernmost tip of the Appalachian Trail. The northernmost point of the trail, Mount Katahdin, is located in the state of Maine, 2,190 miles away. Gatewood threw her denim sling bag over her shoulder and started to hike. She had neither a tent, nor a map, nor a sleeping bag. She was not prepared for the trek and had never done any basic training. For food, she took along canned Vienna sausages, raisins, and peanuts.

There were a lot of things that women didn't usually do in the 1950s in the US, and walking alone through the wilderness was one of them. The Appalachian Trail was not exactly a safe place to wander in the 1950s because of the terrain and the small, isolated communities that were cut off from civilization by an endless stretch of wilderness. Gatewood walked through these untouched places wearing her sling sack and worrying about nothing other than where to lay her head each night—maybe because she felt liberated after having been married for thirty years to a violent man, an alcoholic and impetuous abuser who was finally shot dead in a pub brawl. This event was the turning point in Emma Gatewood's life. In later interviews, she said that she had planned to wait until her children grew up and moved out before she attempted anything. And that's precisely what she did. After her violent husband kicked the bucket and her children moved away from home, Gatewood gathered up her few belongings and started walking on a path that was constructed to be experienced as infinite, as her biographer, Ben Montgomery writes.

Nonetheless. Heroes have a tendency to end up in the headlines. Gatewood might have been unknown when she started, but as she pushed north, rumors spread about the wandering grandma. Journalists interviewed her along the way, and the articles reported that she acquired followers as she went, not unlike Forrest Gump who ends up with a gaggle of newly saved joggers following him on his run across the American continent. Emma Gatewood didn't like all the fuss people were making over her, but she replied politely to the reporters' questions before continuing tirelessly on.

By September of the same year, she stood atop Mount Katahdin. She had achieved what no one had believed possible for a woman her age—or what no one like her had even thought to attempt—and in the course of her trek she became a reluctant national celebrity. She also wore out six pairs of cotton shoes. When her hike was over, she decided to do it again and once she had finished it a second time, she decided to hike the Appalachian Trail a third time, which no one before her had ever done.

That was the last time she hiked the trail. Emma Gatewood died on June 4, 1973. Her daughter later said that her mother had learned about the Appalachian Trail from a magazine article. She had read the article and then said: "If those men can do it, I can do it too."

OF EVERY WALKER I've met, no one has ever left a greater impression on me than Bjørn Amsrud. In 1966, he became the first person to walk the length of Norway, a distance that nowadays holds an almost mythical status in Norwegian hiking circles. I came across the sparsely documented story about him by chance since hardly anything has been written about his trek. Apart from his listed phone number, I was unable to find any information about Amsrud himself.

So I called him up and asked if I could come visit and listen to his stories about his long hike, and he said yes. Amsrud was an old man by then. He had been walking his entire life, but now his knees were giving him problems, he said, and his doctor had recommended taking it easy.

Amsrud was a tall, lean man with large hands, a silver beard, and mild eyes. With his right arm, he leaned on a cane. With his left, he showed me into his sitting room. The shoes he had worn in 1966 were on a shelf in the stairwell. They were made of leather, brown and stiff, with spikes in the soles. Having worn them down over hundreds of miles, he had repaired them himself.

We sat in facing armchairs and started to talk. It was clear that Amsrud was a man of few words but what he told me left an even greater impression.

On June 7, 1966, a young man entered the train station in Oslo. He wore a parka, hiking pants, and brown leather boots. On his back was a green pack. He bought a ticket, went down to the platform, and boarded the train. When he arrived in Kristiansand, he took a bus to Lindesnes, Norway's southernmost point. When he got off the bus, he strapped on his backpack and walked down to the shore. He stuck a finger in the water, turned 180 degrees, and began walking north. A few months later, he would become the first person to walk the entire length of Norway.

Rumors of his accomplishment began to spread through outdoor groups. Not only had Amsrud covered an enormous distance, he had covered it quickly. What's more, he hadn't notified anyone about his expedition beforehand, as most people do these days. He had simply walked, without any press coverage or sponsors, carrying only the most basic equipment.

He was thirty-three years old when he started the trip. He had informed only his direct family members and no one else, as he didn't want to raise expectations prematurely. Amsrud had been an avid walker all his life, and as such he knew that anything could happen en route: injuries or other unforeseen circumstances that might force him to call off the walk. He never asked anyone to join him. He had always walked alone.

He acquired maps from the National Geographical Survey in Oslo, a bulky stack of detailed topographical charts covering Norway in those days. There were large white fields on the maps indicating land that had not yet been surveyed in detail. He tried to follow the paths that had been marked on the maps. They did not always correspond to the terrain, but he nevertheless managed to get through in the end.

Amsrud walked seventeen hundred miles. The landscape shifted constantly, with mountains appearing all the time and making it virtually impossible to walk in a straight line. He learned to read the landscape. He followed the paths he found, and when there were no paths he made his own. As he spoke, I thought that if I were ever to walk across unfamiliar terrain, I would want to choose Amsrud as my pathfinder.

He spoke about what he called his "walking-sensation," a state that comes about from doing nothing other than walking. "When you walk for such a long distance, it becomes a mental experience. You enter into a particular frame of mind that doesn't normally occur in your everyday life. I don't know how else to describe it," Amsrud told me.

On September 10, 1966, he arrived at North Cape, Norway's northernmost point. Here he ended his trip. He was happy to arrive, but as he told me: "I can't say if it's something in our genes. Human beings have always wandered, and if the country had been longer, I would have liked to keep going."

+

EMMA GATEWOOD WOULD never have gone for her long hikes if not for the existence of the long-distance Appalachian Trail. Bjørn Amsrud followed the paths that existed in Norway in the late 1960s, but he also forged his own paths. I imagine that Edward Payson Weston, referred to as "a man in a hurry" by his biographers, was so busy and walked so fast that he hardly stuck to any paths at all.

I often think about these three walkers with a mixture of jealousy and awe. Our modern society is configured in such a way that we can live most of it sitting down. If we spend an hour in a fitness studio once a week, we feel we are exercising enough to stay fit. But something is amiss.

If you walk five miles a day at a normal pace, it will take you nearly two hours. If you do this every day, you will walk a total of thirty miles each week and spend fourteen hours moving, which is fourteen times as much as that single hour at the fitness studio. It's as simple as that. If you make a habit of telling yourself that you're a person who walks—to your job, to school, to the store—you'll end up getting all the exercise your body needs without even thinking about it. You will merely be doing what you were born to do.

Infants are born unable to lift their heads or bodies, but when they are only a few months old they slowly start to develop the strength and control needed to do this. First, they wriggle forward on their bellies and then they start to crawl. By the time they are around a year old, they are able to pull themselves up and start walking. Their legs are stiff and they struggle to keep their balance. Their little bodies—big head, short arms and legs, soft, rounded feet—are not yet proportioned for walking. They have not yet grown into their final form. As they grow older, their style of walking changes. They slowly begin to walk more upright, their feet grow stronger and flatter, their toes point down instead of up and learn to grip the floor. By the time they are small children, their knee joints bend and they find a balancing point. In this way, they walk through life until they grow old, until their back starts to bend forward, their balance falters, their muscles grow weaker, and their life as a walking being reaches an end.

That's how it is for all of us. But there's one thing I'm dead certain of: I will keep walking until I can walk no farther. After that, I will sit in a chair and think about when I used to be able to walk. I'll shut my eyes and feel the shift of weight from one foot to the other: how one foot lands on its heel and rolls forward, how the toes kick off at the same second when the other foot lands, how the arms create momentum, moving in the opposite direction as my legs, left arm forward, right leg back, thigh muscles and leg muscles pushing my body onward, spine straight, head raised, my gaze fixed on what's ahead.

INNER
LANDSCAPES

THE FIRST PATHS we ever took, why do they stay with us our entire lives?

A path in the countryside, in the city, at the sea, in the forest, one we walked so often that it became a part of us. A route to school, through the neighborhood park, into a patch of woods, across a field. A shortcut to the convenience store, the soccer field, the beach, a friend's house. A path we knew in every kind of weather and at every time of year, which was a part of us in a way that only children can know because children live in close contact with the earth, down low where the asphalt, roots, cigarette butts, flowers, chocolate wrappers, soda caps, and ants all are.

Childhood paths are recollections of the body's contact with the outside world. Small feet across the earth's
surface. This is why we never forget them.

THE CABIN OF my childhood sits in an elevated clearing with a view out over a large lake. A gravel road
winds along the shore of the lake. It disappears behind
a mountain, and behind the mountain is the farm
that was my mother's childhood home. Grandma and
Grandpa had horses and cows, pigs and hens, fields of
potatoes and vegetables. The farm was still in operation
at the time of my birth.

The farm was first built and the fields cleared as
far back as the 1400s. The ground was broken up by
human hands once long ago, trees were felled, stones
carted away. Several of the fields were located deep
within the forest. They were always small fields; none of
them were ever big. "Upon inspection of farm no.1748,
it is noted that the soil is dry and rocky and no more
soil can be cleared," states the village district's record
book. It is a meager, rugged landscape that is difficult to
farm. Nothing came without a cost for the farmers. The
annual yield depended on the weather and the amount
of labor that was put into it.

My grandfather's relatives had lived on the farm
since 1896. My great-great-grandparents had purchased

it from the region's big forest owner. My grandmother's family lived on a farm a few miles away through the forest along a cart track. My grandparents were married in the spring of 1946, a year after the Second World War ended and Norway once again became a free and independent nation. They had three children: my mother first, then my aunt, and finally my uncle. They moved to the farm where my grandfather was the sole heir and there they stayed.

Grandma looked after the animals while Grandpa tended the fields. In the winter, he took to the forest to cut down trees along the many paths that wound through it. It was a hard life. They had to earn a living to support themselves and their children, but they also had to be able to feed their animals, and this is how the path behind the cabin came into being.

THE PATH BEGAN at the cabin and led up to a field that lay deep within the forest. The field had been cleared by the big forest owner once in the 1800s before my great-great-grandparents bought the land, and so they took over the field. The forest owner had transported logs out of the forest, and once the trees were felled, the light was able to get through. Tall grass grew up in the little field, and this grass would get my family through the summer. Everyone helped out: Grandma,

Grandpa, my mother, aunt, and uncle. They strung up the grass on racks to dry in the sun, and when it was dry enough they went to get it with a horse and wagon and took it back to the farm and into the barn to feed the cows and horses throughout the winter.

The constant movement to and from the field meant that the path never grew over. Horse hooves, wagon wheels, and human feet, the path was maintained by labor and it wasn't until many years later, when I was growing up, that the sole purpose of the path became walking.

NOW TWO ENTIRE generations of my family are gone, people who passed their lives in this place. My great-great-grandparents, who died long before I was born. After them came my great-grandparents, who died when I was a little boy and who I therefore cannot remember other than from black-and-white photos. In those images they are old weatherworn folks sitting in chairs or standing in a field, men with hats, women with large heavy dresses, all of them with furrowed faces marked by a life lived outside.

Grandpa lived in the fields and he died in them too. I can still remember the day he was buried. I was thirteen and it was the middle of summer. He was buried in a little churchyard in the nearest town. I can't remember anything about the priest's eulogy, but I do remember the cold church hall, the wood-paneled walls, and the smell of dust and flowers. When we went outside onto the church steps after the ceremony, the burial procession paused. I stood alone on those stairs. I couldn't see my mother or father and sisters among all of the people in their best clothes. As I stood there, I overheard a conversation between some men who were also farmers and old friends of my grandparents. When they stepped out of the church, all of them immediately turned their faces toward the sky. It was blue and clear outside, a beautiful summer's day. They looked up at the sky, and then they started discussing the weather, as farmers do. They spoke about the weather as if nothing had happened. They didn't seem to notice me standing there listening, and I remember thinking: my grandpa and your good friend for over half a century hasn't even been buried yet, and here you are already discussing the weather. It didn't make any sense to me, standing there; there was something outrageous about the situation, something deeply confusing. I felt the rage welling up in me but I didn't know what to say, so I turned around and left while the sobs caught in my throat. Since then, I've come to understand that this is how farmers were in those days, and it's how farmers are now. If one of those men on the stairs had died, my grandfather would have been the one standing there discussing the weather. Everything pivoted around their work and the harvest. Life goes on, even when someone departs from it.

$$+$$

AS A CHILD, I dreamed about perfect landscapes and I composed them whenever I drew. The boys at school drew pictures of low-slung cars with big wheels and race numbers painted across the sides. The girls drew portraits of other girls. The boys drew their cars to be as cool as possible and filled the page with clouds of black exhaust. The girls made their portraits as sweet as possible, exaggerating the size of the eyes and lips and earlobes to the same extent that the boys exaggerated the amount of vehicle exhaust.

Cars didn't interest me, and neither did girls, so I drew landscapes instead. My landscape pictures were always devoid of people and rendered in green, brown, black, and blue. They were confined and obvious, always a variation on the landscape around the little cabin. The drawings contained the most important components of a classical cultural landscape: forest, farm, lake, and path. As the landscape architect, I positioned the different elements across the page, and the path was in the middle. It was what connected the forest, lake, and farm. It wound through the terrain, taking neither the shortest nor simplest way between two points but the opposite. My path was deeply irrational when it came to saving energy, because I made sure to give it as many twists and turns as possible. The more turns it has, the more path there is, was my way of thinking. The path was always winding, even over terrain that appeared totally flat and could easily have accommodated a straight line. I drew curvy lines. Straight lines were something I associated with paved roads, and paved roads were what the car-loving boys liked.

EVERYTHING THAT HAPPENS must happen in a place. Famous battles, romantic rendezvous, decisive soccer matches, important pacts or agreements. Each event is anchored in a landscape and so is our memory. "Took place," we say. We don't remember abstract ideas so much as we do our physical surroundings. If you have ever been dumped by someone, you may not remember exactly what they said or precisely which words they used, but you will most certainly remember where you were when they said it.

I have always imagined that playwright William Shakespeare's famous line "All the world's a stage" is about precisely this idea.

All the world's a stage,
And all the men and women merely players;
They have their exits and their entrances,
And one man in his time plays many parts.

This quote may be about something completely different, but I don't really care. The way I understand these lines, they are not so much about the roles we play as they are about where we play them. Every event occurs in a place, a scene in which we are the participants. Later on, the scenes are what we remember because every single event is so inextricably linked to its surrounding that it cannot be recalled independent of it. Arne Næss, who never walked the same route to his cabin Tvergastein so as not to make a path, expressed this idea in *Life's Philosophy*: I don't distinguish very sharply between myself and the cabin. The way he saw it, the man Arne Næss and his cabin were merely two sides of the same coin.

The ideas of French philosopher Maurice Merleau-Ponty hash out the theoretical foundations of Annette Bischoff's doctoral dissertation on paths, in particular the emphasis on the body's role in our world of experience. We are in the world, the philosopher implies, and it is only here where we are able to know ourselves. Merleau-Ponty's words call to mind the experience of walking on a path through a landscape. You are there, and that is your whole world, he says. Bischoff writes:

> *The basic conditions of human existence are the corporeal presence in the world...We are immersed in the world and the world is taken in through our bodies. We walk on paths, and the surroundings are sensed through our bodies, the wind against our skin, the sun on our face, the ground beneath our feet: boulders, gravel, grass, sand, roots, stones.*

Maybe the landscape was always changing for nomadic Stone Age humans. Maybe Stone Age peoples weren't tied to a specific geographical area but to the landscape as such. Maybe it was only after the agricultural revolution, when humans settled down, that humans' connection to a particular landscape grew so strong and determinative to their identity that it has become more important than gender, religion, language, culture, and social classifications. Just think of the word "homesickness" and the little embroidered "Home sweet home" pictures that are always hanging in kitchens in the movies.

There are the places we miss. New Yorkers living in San Francisco miss New York more than they miss other New Yorkers. Canadians miss Canada. Italians miss Italy. Chileans miss Chile. Anyone who must flee from their homeland knowing they might never see it again, who will they be for the rest of their lives when they can no longer return to where they came from?

Henrik Ibsen wrote *Peer Gynt,* a play set in Norway, while living in Italy. Knut Hamsun wrote *Pan,* a tragic drama played out in the Norwegian woods, while living in Paris. There are dozens of love songs that have been written over time about specific places. "Sweet Home Alabama." "Georgia on My Mind." "New York, New York." "I Left My Heart in San Francisco." Maybe Arne Næss was right. Maybe the intimacy between humans and places exists because they are not sharply distinguishable from each other.

When I spoke with Kenneth Buch, Norway's national orienteering team coach, he told me it is remarkably advantageous for runners to compete on their home turf. It isn't only that a Swiss runner benefits if the competition is held in Switzerland. The Swiss team members will also have varying degrees of advantage depending on where the competition is held. A runner from the particular district in Switzerland where the competition is taking place will have a much stronger advantage than runners from other countries and even from other regions of Switzerland.

WHEN IT COMES to our memories of landscapes, it makes a significant difference whether you are an adult or a child. An adult knows where the landscape is located, how large it is, and what type of natural features one might expect to find there. A child knows none of this. They don't possess any knowledge about the landscape. They cannot place it in a larger context or compare it with other landscapes. For a child, this one landscape is all they have, and in this way, this landscape is the only thing in the world.

When a child gets older, they start to see it differently. The creek, the mountain, the forest, the lake. They start to understand everything, to ascribe words to it, and that original landscape becomes one among many.

This process is how the world is demystified, and this is perhaps why we shouldn't try to seek out childhood paths in order to walk them again. What could we possibly gain by doing so? You might discover that the place that formed you as a person and which you experienced as magical is, in reality, nothing more than a completely ordinary place. Yet, is it perhaps precisely in the ordinary that the magic lies? Is this what we forget with age? Is this, in fact, why we sometimes feel wistful and nostalgic as adults? Why we experience a longing for a time that was simpler and more concrete than the one we inhabit as grown-ups? A longing for a child's eye for details and their ability to lose themselves in the commonplace?

+

MY GRANDMOTHER LIVED for many decades after my grandfather's death. She was the last of her generation. I regretted that I never sat with her and asked her to tell me the story of her life from beginning to end, about her and my grandpa, the farm, the place, and the path behind the cabin.

She was born just after the First World War and was almost ninety when she died. She was part of a generation that lived through an evolution that's nearly impossible to grasp. She began her life with horses and wagons and ended it with cars and highways and great-grandchildren downloading apps on their smartphones. She lived her entire life on a farm beside a lake, almost five miles from the nearest town.

Grandma was worried about ending up in a nursing home. She never said it out loud, but her message got through nonetheless: I wish to live here until I die.

She never ended up in the nursing home. She remained healthy until she got sick, and then she died. She was buried next to my grandfather in the little churchyard in the nearest town. After the service, we held a small memorial in a little white assembly hall on a hilltop, with views of the farm and the lake and the surrounding terrain.

We ate stew and drank coffee and talked about Grandma. This side of the family always eats stew regardless of whether we are marking births or deaths; it is a tradition handed down to us by Grandma. Grandma's children gave speeches. The grandchildren listened. Her great-grandchildren ran around as if nothing had happened. Everyone was there. The only person missing was Grandma.

I went outside. I looked out across the landscape where her life had unfolded, all of her days, all of her years, and I thought how strange it was this place could still exist without her. In the context of the landscape, her life had been only a fleeting moment, but for me, she had always been there. The place was inseparably linked to Grandma; it could not be imagined without her within it, and I think that's how she must have seen it too. She could not picture herself without also picturing the farm. She could not imagine who she might have been without that place.

PART
IV

BACK WHERE
I STARTED

ONE YEAR HAD passed since I parked the Volvo and started to walk. Over the course of the year, I had gradually changed and now, standing on the threshold of a new spring, I felt that something material had shifted. I had become a new person, or I had become a very old person, a wandering figure who had not moved forward in time but back, toward the past and my nomadic ancestors.

If there was somewhere I needed to go, I went there on foot. I always wore a backpack. It was filled with everyday items: books, things I needed at the office, and other objects. There was always something I needed to transport from one place to another. Even when I didn't need my backpack to carry anything,

I still brought it with me. I felt naked without that back-pack. It had become a part of my body, as if I were a dromedary and the backpack was my hump.

The winter came to an end. The light returned. Migratory birds flew in across the country, and the paths that had been lying dormant beneath piles of snow for four months began once again to reveal themselves.

This was the moment I'd been waiting for, and on the first day of May I decided it was finally time. The forest was saturated with the snowmelt of winter. Where it was shady, the snow was piled knee-deep, but I took a chance that the paths would be accommodating enough. Or rather, the path, for this time it was not just any path that I was planning to walk. It was The Path, as though that was its name, written in capital letters, in definite form and singular: the path behind our cabin, the path in my life.

+

MY CHILDHOOD CABIN is located far away from people. I had always gone there by car, but now the epilepsy prevented me from driving and I didn't want to ask anyone for a ride. I researched if public transport could get me there, a local bus or train, but there was none. My only alternative, then, was to go on foot, and yet I could not walk all the way from Oslo without it taking me a week at least. Instead, I decided to walk to the cabin from the closest train station, which was in Larvik. From there, it would still be a good stretch to the cabin, but at least I could walk through empty forested areas instead of along a paved road full of cars.

It was evening by the time I filled my backpack and said goodbye to my family. I knew it would take me about an hour to walk from my home to Oslo Central Station, and as I ascended the final steps to the station and stood in front of the large digital screen flashing the departure and arrival times, I felt deeply satisfied to see that I had timed my walk perfectly.

I left the city on the evening's last southbound train, and when the train stopped in Larvik a few hours later I got off. The evening was wet and chilly. The rain caused the asphalt to gleam like the newly polished hood of an expensive car. Puddles mirrored light from the street lamps.

I booked myself into a hotel. The hotel was spacious and empty, and for all I knew I was the only guest. I was given a key card and found my way to the room I had reserved. I dumped the contents of my backpack onto the floor and spread them out. A windbreaker. Rain gear and extra socks. A fleece jacket and hiking pants.

A wool sweater, shorts, coffee, a camp stove. A map and compass. A knife. A cup. A bit of food. A camera.

I lay on the bed studying the map. Directly north of Larvik, a half-hour walk from the hotel, was the big lake that we had been able to see from my childhood cabin. The lake was long and narrow. It stretched from south to north. Larvik was in the south, the small cabin at the north end. The map showed a network of hiking trails through the forested area along the eastern side of the lake. The paths were marked in red and led in all different directions. I didn't recognize any of them but I knew that if I simply headed north, they would lead me all the way to the cabin.

I set the alarm on my phone for four a.m. Before falling asleep, I ran through my plan one last time. I would walk from sunup to sundown through a forest I didn't know and on paths I had never taken. Measured out on the terrain, the distance was no more than twelve to twenty miles. I would need to adjust my tempo to the distance I would be walking, and since I wanted to walk for at least a half day before reaching the cabin, I would need to walk very slowly. This thought had appealed to me more and more since the idea had first occurred to me a few weeks earlier. Everything in our culture is focused on the fastest; nothing is about striving to be the slowest. I felt like the foremost pioneer of walking.

I planned to walk as slowly as possible for an entire day, and for all I knew, I was the first person ever to have such an idea.

This was my plan. I would start at sunup and walk until sundown. When I arrived at the cabin, I would stay the night. The next morning, I would walk the small path. I would find out if it was still as I remembered it, if it was even there at all, or if it had long ago been swallowed up by the surrounding landscape.

✦

I WOKE UP to my alarm clock ringing. Sleep clung like intoxication, unwilling to let go. I reluctantly got out of bed and pulled open the curtains. It was still dark outside the hotel window but the rain had stopped. I packed my bag and went down to reception. The receptionist seemed disappointed and amazed that the hotel's only guest planned to check out when it was still dark. I would gladly have slept another few hours just to make her happy, but I had a task to do and a forest ahead of me.

I left the hotel and ambled slowly through the empty streets of Larvik. The town slept; only the gulls were on the wing. I came to a peaceful beech forest within which were the remains of an old path that I wanted to check out before continuing on. The Vikings had once lived here. These mysterious warriors and their small sturdy horses left behind paths, sunken lanes, tracks from over a thousand years ago.

Sunken lanes, or holloways as they are also called, are distinctive walking and riding paths that date as far back as 500 BC. They can be found all over Europe. They got their name because the traffic on these paths was so heavy that deep, tunnel-like grooves formed— so deep that some people preferred walking or riding on the embankment instead of at the base of the path.

The beech forest of Larvik is a popular hiking area in Norway. Signs with information about the history, geology, and fauna of the landscape line the many paths that have been formed. I read all of them with great interest but it was the holloway I wanted to see, and after a little bit of searching I found it. It was signposted too. If it had not been, I would have walked right past it.

Once I had noticed it, the sunken depression along the forest floor was easy to identify. It was covered by a thick layer of rotting leaves, but it was nonetheless visible as an indentation, seven feet wide, two feet deep. The Vikings had walked here. I pictured them, a procession of silent, filthy men with swords and shields, helmets on their heads and long, unkempt beards. I knew this was a simplified vision that perhaps did not give the Vikings the credit they deserved. I knew in reality that their culture was much more diverse, but the historical fate of the Vikings has long since been sealed and they will always be known as a brutal and warlike folk.

On the other side of the beech forest, only a few hundred yards from where I stood, was a four-lane highway and just beyond that was the big lake. The highway had recently been expanded and modernized to meet the standards expected by today's drivers. It was the lights from this highway that John and I saw when we paddled out onto the lake that winter night thirty years ago. Now I pictured the motorists on this early spring morning. Descendants of the Vikings, descendants of nomads, people sitting behind the wheel of their expensive automobiles, commuters in uniforms and suits on their way into the city, to important meetings in the finance or information tech sectors.

I saw the newly upgraded highway between the ancient beech trunks and I was overcome by a peculiar feeling. Here I stood with one foot in the past and one in the present. From a holloway to a highway in ten minutes. Vikings and financiers. One old path and one new. A thousand years' time. Light-years of evolution.

A small gravel path led beneath the highway. I followed it and when I emerged on the other side, I saw

the forests and the big lake. I walked out onto a promontory. Beams of sunlight fell on my neck and cast a
gleaming white light across the surface of the water.
The city and the highway lay behind me; the landscape
and the paths lay ahead. I pulled my backpack onto my
shoulders and began to walk. I felt free and happy. I
was on the threshold of a small adventure, a miniature
journey of discovery. I did not know where I was, but
I knew where I was going. The path through the town
was only a prologue. The true start of my long trip to
the cabin began from this point on.

IF I HAD lived 10,000 years ago, during the Mesolithic
period, the second era of the Stone Age, I would have
belonged to a small group of people, a clan of perhaps
ten or twenty individuals. We would have been the first
humans in a landscape in which no other human beings
had ever set foot. Haphazard and ambiguous, formed
by the heedless ice.

If we had been the first people in a place such as that,
what would we have done?

We would have found a good camping spot and
built a shelter. We would have made sure our camping
spot was protected from rain and wind, close to water,
and with a view out across the surrounding terrain. We
would have looked for food, hunted, and gathered. For

this, we would have required weapons and some simple tools. We would thus have looked for trees from which to form the shafts of arrows and the handles of axes, and stones that could work as the arrowheads and axe bits. If we had managed to kill a deer, we could have used the bones and horns to craft additional tools: knives and fishing hooks from the bones, and fishing line and sewing thread from the muscle tendons. We would have collected fuel to light a bonfire. Fire was vital in a world that was cold, even when temperatures rose.

We would have familiarized ourselves with the terrain and soon, just like all other living beings, we would have formed habits. We would have traced the same arc each time we went out to hunt, gather, fish, or collect fuel. I would have followed the others and the others would have followed me. We would have trusted in each other's choices and soon there would have been small arteries through the terrain, paths embodying our choices, which would not only have simplified our movement but also guided us back to the camping spot if one of us got lost.

We would have stayed at the camping spot for a while. When resources ran low, or when our quarry moved on, we would have broken camp and continued. We would have taken with us the few objects we possessed: leather clothes, our spear, the fishhooks, and the axe. We would have continued north. Driven by survival and the urge to explore, we would have analyzed the terrain and staked out a course into the unknown landscape.

None of the paths left by humans of the Stone Age still exist today. None of the paths that were created before the Stone Age do either. All of them vanished long ago because the landscapes in which they were formed have become altered unrecognizably by earthquakes, meteorites, storms, floods, volcanoes, ice ages, and continental flow. But that they did exist is certain, ever since our earliest relatives, the so-called *Ardipithecus*, climbed down from trees on Africa's savannahs almost six million years ago and were followed by *Australopithecus, Homo habilis, Homo rudolfensis, Homo erectus, Homo heidelbergensis, Homo neanderthalensis,* and finally us, *Homo sapiens.*

From a biogenetic perspective, the *Ardipithecus* are our closest link to primates and to those who took their first steps on two legs, thereby heralding one of humankind's primary advantages for existence: bipedal movement.

Humans walk on two legs, and from an evolutionary perspective, this way of moving has proved an advantage on par with our large brains. When we started walking upright, we freed up our arms and thereby our hands. This meant we could now carry our own off-spring and move both as a group and more rapidly.

For thousands of years, bipedal movement contributed to the evolution of our hands. What were once front legs developed into sophisticated grippers with unsurpassed motor skills. The dexterity of our fingers was slowly refined to perfection. And the development of the fine motor skills in our fingers has been a crucial step in human evolution: it has allowed us to form and create advanced tools.

Our closest relative, the chimpanzee, is also partially bipedal, but the chimpanzee nonetheless moves more often on four legs. Chimpanzees still live in trees and therefore depend first and foremost on hands that can grasp branches and stems. There is a clear difference between our hands and those of the chimpanzee. The thumb of chimpanzees is in line with their other fingers and leans in the same direction, while our thumb is separate from our other fingers and turns inward. This physiological trait is called an "opposable thumb" and has made us unique among species. With our opposable thumb, we are able to embroider a doily with small intricate loops or pull a length of thin fishing line through the tiny eye of a lure. We can hold a pencil and write with it. We are able to brush minute details into a painting. We can develop elaborate tools and advanced microtechnology. One of the first things a newborn child does is grasp its parents' fingers with its entire hand, and when it is only six or seven months old, it learns to lift and hold an object between its thumb and index finger, a developmental milestone known as the "pincer grasp."

LEAVING THE CITY and the highway behind me, I continued along the shore of the lake. The path was wide and smooth. Birdsong rose with the morning light. It rose like a symphony builds toward a crescendo, and unseen insects buzzed on the forest floor. I wandered along like a brooding philosopher, looked to my right and to my left, stopped, turned, and then kept going. I walked so slowly that I was barely moving. At the end of my life this is going to be my pace, so I might as well prepare for it now, I thought. I was the snail at Mistaken Point, and with every footfall I felt happier and happier about it. How slowly can one move through a whole day? How much time can one take to cover a distance? I had thought up a brand-new concept, the antithesis of competitive sports, and it made me feel proud and content.

Time passed slowly, as time should. I got hungry. I went down to the lake and found a spot sheltered from the wind. I put the coffee pot on the stove and checked my watch. It was eleven. I took out the map. It showed that I had walked for two-and-a-half miles.

This was the way I used to walk as a child, me and everyone else. We would walk, stop, turn around, walk back, keep going, rest, and turn around again. It was true what we told our parents whenever we missed dinner. "I forgot the time!" we would say. We simply never stopped to think about the time that was passing or where we were going. Walking without a goal was the most natural thing in the world. To walk in a straight line seemed meaningless. To walk quickly seemed meaningless. I can still remember the feeling of my own short legs trying to keep up with an adult who was in a hurry and taking long strides.

COMPARED TO THE humans who lived farther south, the Stone Age people in northern Europe had almost nothing. No knowledge, no written language, no maps, no simple tools. But in one skill they were at least as good as their southern relatives: their ability to navigate.

They walked toward the ice. They moved through a bleak and fruitless landscape, a stone desert that must have got colder and more sparse the farther north they moved. They had no idea what might meet them there, no concept or expectation handed down from older members of the tribe or from other clans, nothing to prepare them for what they would face. And still they kept walking.

For the humans of the Stone Age, life was one great migration from birth to death. Life was a journey, not figuratively but literally. There was no such thing as home, and thus no homesickness. There was no method of survival other than simply moving on. In *A Field Guide to Getting Lost*, Rebecca Solnit writes that movement was essential for survival and that remaining in one place was tantamount to committing suicide.

The term "ice age" describes a period in the history of the earth when the average temperature plummeted and the ice-covered regions in the north and south spread and grew, creeping toward the middle of the globe, toward the equator.

Since its birth 4.6 billion years ago, the earth has experienced many ice ages. Large ones and small ones, long and short. The last ice age continued for over a hundred thousand years. It began between a hundred thousand and fifty thousand years after humans began their exploration of the globe.

Scientists assume that the ice in the northern hemisphere during the last glacial period reached all the way down to Central Europe and the middle of the North American continent to about the same latitude where

Frankfurt and Seattle are located today. Ice covered everything and never melted. Humans lived at the edge of the ice and in toward the equator.

The ice melted and the ocean rose, but the land masses rose even more. The weight of the ice had compressed the crust of the earth, but when the crust lifted, it rose and bulged in places and created the landscape we know today.

I NOW FOUND myself only a dozen miles or so from where the edge of the ice must have been eleven thousand years ago. The landscape back then was dominated by gravel and stone. There was scant vegetation, no tall trees, nothing but scattered dwarf birches and the dwarf willow and sea buckthorn bushes, which were among the first forms of vegetation to come to this region.

Not only was such landscape unfamiliar to people of the Stone Age, it was also undergoing massive changes. The land rose so quickly that it may have shifted in appearance from one generation to the next. What knowledge did humans have to develop to navigate such a shifting landscape? What knowledge did they have to pass on to their children to help them survive? They could not simply say, as we do: "follow that path," or "that is a good camping spot." Such knowledge was nontransferable because neither the path nor the camping spot would be there in a generation or two. Humans of the Stone Age must have possessed a general wisdom about the landscape's characteristics rather than a knowledge of its concrete locations. And this information must have been crucial for the survival of individuals and cultures.

WALKING SLOWLY IS an understated art. I tried as I walked to find the perfect tempo and the perfect rhythm. I could feel my feet working, how each foot would land on the heel and roll forward and kick off with the toes. Even my little toes were working, these strange anatomical details that seem both malformed and superfluous.

When Peter Christen Asbjørnsen and Jørgen Engebretsen Moe—the Norwegian brothers Grimm— collected fairy tales, they did so by walking from place to place, along paths and wagon tracks, in search of people who might be familiar with the folktales that were rarely written down but had been handed down orally from generation to generation. I'm convinced that Asbjørnsen and Moe must have walked slowly. It's impossible to imagine that they would have walked fast because they needed to gain the trust of those they met along the way in order to gain access to their stories. Asbjørnsen and Moe must have known that no one trusts busy people who rush around without taking in their surroundings. That is why they must have walked slowly.

Fairy tales came into existence through movement, and they were collected through movement. Initially, the stories were passed from mouth to mouth; later, Asbjørnsen and Moe gathered them as they passed from village to village. Until that moment when the stories were written down, they had developed and changed, the way it always is with stories that are passed along orally. Stories are embellished by the storyteller, who leaves something out or adds something in. A path is no different. Those who walk on a path follow its main impression, but every now and then they deviate from it, not by very much perhaps, but a little; for example, when the path is flooded after a heavy downpour or when a tree has fallen across it. Paths and folktales both evolve over time. They are never static; they are always shifting, influenced by the people who walk or retell them. As far as the fairy tales are concerned, this constant evolution gives them greater value as folklore, though less credibility as truth and reality. Fairy tales are said to have come "through the grapevine," an expression that is now almost synonymous with "gossip" and thus makes them less credible and also less reputable. This modern understanding implies they promote ideas that can be construed as untrue, or even malicious.

The path is reminiscent of folktales both in its essence and in its creation. No single person is responsible for a path; instead, it is the sum of the actions of numerous people over a period of time that dates back to the distant past. As such, paths are like stories. Both constitute a movement from a beginning to an end, and they both have a middle. In storytelling, this mid-point is the moment in the story when the plot gains momentum. On the path, it is called the halfway point. Many of us think of it as the *point of no return*, because from this point on there's no sense in turning around; we might as well continue to the end of the path.

I PAUSED FOR the second break in my walk that day, even though I didn't need one. I was neither tired nor hungry. It seemed that my remarkably slow pace was allowing my body to recover even as I walked, as if the energy I was expending by walking was simultaneously renewed by the surrounding landscape and my exceptionally good mood. I thought about the Australian aborigines and a book I had just finished reading, written by the well-known travel book writer Bruce Chatwin. The book is called *The Songlines*, and it is about the ancient aboriginal trails in the Australian outback. The trails are not visible in the traditional sense, but they are linked to specific landmarks about which the ancestors have sung.

The aborigines sing their paths into existence, and Chatwin wanted to understand more about these songlines. When I had finished reading his book from cover to cover, I was still uncertain whether Chatwin had been able to grasp the concept, and I didn't quite grasp it myself, but it has something to do with an oral tradition of both spiritual and cultural understanding, as well as the art of the landscape. In this sense, a songline is similar to a folktale.

The aborigines have a rite of passage called a "walkabout." It is an ancient practice undertaken by young aborigines to mark the transition from childhood to adulthood. Those who practice walkabout are in "temporary mobility"; they are nomadic for a period of time, and journey alone through the vast, blazing wilderness of the Australian outback. The purpose of walkabout is for young people to gain the skills necessary for survival, but it is also about something larger, something having to do with identity and history. Walking through the landscape of their ancestors, following the songlines and the paths their elders once made, these young aborigines are able to commune with their traditional, spiritual roots.

Chatwin describes the aboriginal songlines as a "labyrinth of invisible paths," "a spaghetti of Iliads and Odysseys." Before they were displaced and assimilated by white Europeans, all young aborigines went on a walkabout along such songlines. They would follow in their ancestors' footsteps and sing their songs. It was a journey through time and space in which the goal was insight and the journey was the mode. To this end, a pair of strong feet was of utmost value for the aborigines.

LIFE ON THE path was simple. I saw a roe deer behind the dense tangle of leafless branches. It stood completely motionless, gazing at me. For all I knew, it could have been standing there for quite a while but when I turned my head and the roe deer saw my eyes and realized it had been discovered, it disappeared without a sound, as if God took a breath and blew it carefully away.

I saw stumps left by a beaver along the shore of the lake. Tooth marks everywhere. Clear paths where the beaver had its favored routes into and out of the water, visible proof of its unwavering work ethic.

I saw brown trout darting in and out of a creek's excavated tunnels. I heard a woodpecker several hundred yards away. The knocking sounded like the stutter of a machine gun in the midst of the quiet forest. The deciduous trees wore small green buds and islands of white anemones covered the forest floor. I walked and observed, walked and observed. The landscape around me shifted and transformed continuously.

MOVEMENT IS IMPORTANT for humans. "Like a rolling stone," we say. When we are not moving, we say we are "bogged down" or "mired" or that we've "ground to a halt," all of which have negative connotations. We associate a lack of movement with a lack of development and growth, with decay and death.

In *Pilgrim at Tinker Creek*, writer Annie Dillard claims that the fixed makes us afraid. What she means by this, if I understand her correctly, is that movement and intentional mobility in a particular direction are such a fundamental part of what it means to be human that the opposite—the experience of standing still, of being nailed to the spot—feels unbearable, almost inhuman. Maybe this is why all people, regardless of culture, gender, religion, or class, have had a nightmare at one point or another in which they are running but cannot seem to move an inch. Maybe this is why the trolls of Norwegian fairy tales turn to stone, because we can think of no harsher punishment than being fixed in place for all eternity.

Even if folklore about mischievous and unfriendly trolls or ogres no longer unnerves people as it used to, there are still traces in our culture that hint at our fear of restricted movement. Rather than limiting a person's opinions, religion, or thought, our criminal justice system—in one of the most frightening aspects of our modern democracy—punishes wrongdoing by limiting a person's freedom of movement. We sentence people to prison, to remain in a strictly constrained environment in which they cannot move around freely. In this regard, there is a certain irony to the fact that a society that considers restricted movement one of the harshest forms of punishment for its citizens simultaneously considers battery cages and other confined spaces that are hardly distinguishable from prison as perfectly acceptable forms of shelter for animals.

One common argument from advocates of zoos is that many of the animals were born in captivity and therefore are not missing an unrestricted way of life. This argument assumes that all of our needs, those of animals as well as humans, are learned through socialization. That a brown bear teaching her young to cover enormous distances in search of food is the reason they continue to do it all their lives. And yet, this is not how things actually work. We do learn some things from our parents, but not everything. A motherless young brown bear will wander for food without ever having learned to do it. The arctic tern will fly. The wild reindeer will run. The eel will swim. If a human is born in a room and confined to that room for the rest of their life, they will long for something they cannot quite put to words, but which is nonetheless a full longing, and that longing—that sense that something is not as it should be—will lead them to apathy and depression.

The brown bear covers enormous distances, and it does so because it possesses something innate that says this is what it is to be a brown bear. Its persistent wandering is a part of the nature of a brown bear; it is one of its most powerful instincts. It is through wandering that a bear realizes itself, which is why a bear held in captivity will continue to walk around and around; it is trying to satisfy its natural urge to wander inside a space that is miniscule compared to the open landscape in which it would normally live its life. If we can appreciate this fact, we can also appreciate how grotesque a tradition it really is to keep animals locked up in cages.

Another illustration that constrained mobility is among the worst possible punishments for humans can be found in *The Divine Comedy* by the fourteenth-century poet Dante Alighieri. The poem relates Dante's journey through the three realms of the dead, first down in Hell, then through Purgatory, and finally up in Paradise. Accompanying him is Dante's great hero, the Roman poet Virgil. In one of the best-known cantos, Virgil and Dante descend to the Second Circle of Hell, where the lustful souls—those who have given in to the desires of the flesh during their lifetime—are held. Cleopatra is there, Helen of Troy, Achilles, Paris, Tristan. The two poets also meet a woman by the name of Francesca da Rimini and her lover, Paolo. The couple carried on an affair while they were alive, but Francesca's husband surprised them in the middle of their lovemaking and killed them both. *The Divine Comedy* is a deeply Christian work of poetry, and unfaithfulness in marriage is considered a great sin. Because Francesca and Paolo gave in to their fleshly lusts, their desires for something corporeal and perishable, they have been condemned to whirling in circles on an eternal blast of wind. The core of this punishment, the truly unbearable nature of it, is that the two lovers will never be able to escape this whirlwind (except for the brief respite when they tell their story to Dante and Virgil) and that the whirlwind never leads to anything.

THE WORLD BECOMES an enchanted and open place when we travel on foot, claims the German filmmaker

Werner Herzog, and he's right. The deeper I walked into the forest, the more apparent it seemed to me that speed and perspective are proportionately opposite. A person who walks slowly sees much, and a person who walks quickly sees little. A person who is running as quickly as possible has their attention focused on their own body. Whereas the attention of a person walking slowly is aimed away from themselves, toward the world and everything outside.

In addition, the difference between walking alone and walking in the company of others is so great that it can hardly be exaggerated. It doesn't matter whether there is only one friend or a group of twenty. Alone or not alone, that is the question. When you walk alone, there are no discussions and the only sound is your feet landing on the path. You will even instinctively try to limit these noises. When you walk alone, you walk quietly without even noticing it. You wish to not disturb and to not be noticed, and this extra caution has the side effect that you also see and hear more of what is going on around you. Walking on a path through a wooded area, you may think there's nothing there; however, if you stop and stand completely still, you will slowly begin to realize how wrong you are. Life is everywhere: there are birds in the trees, insects in the air, ants on the ground, every manner of living being—great and small. They are aware of your presence.

They can hear and smell you. They can see you, but you may not see them.

IF THERE IS one narrative archetype that appears more frequently than any other in Western story traditions—and quite possibly in those from around the world—it must be the hero's journey. The journey might take place in the real universe or in a fictional one. It may be undertaken on foot, by boat, or on a horse, or in our own era, by car, as in Jack Kerouac's beloved novel *On the Road*. Homer's *The Odyssey* and *The Iliad* use the journey as their overarching structure. *The Divine Comedy* is a journey through the realms of death, and Miguel de Cervantes's classic novel, *Don Quixote*, is a journey via horse and donkey through the Spanish landscape.

In the last half of the 1600s, "voyages of discovery" became a popular phenomenon among the European upper class. The most important formula of such a voyage of discovery was that the traveler should expand their horizons, preferably to either Italy or France, the great epicenters of culture. Many such voyages were later turned into stories. One trait of these stories is that they are less about the destination than about the journey itself, the state of voyaging. At the center of almost all such stories is what befalls the hero along the way. Modern interrail and backpacking adventures are the discovery voyages of our day and age. Young people set off to travel across the globe, and when they get back home, they have acquired important knowledge about other cultures and learned something they would never have learned merely by staying home.

In the delightful little story *Travels with a Donkey in the Cévennes*, author Robert Louis Stevenson, who is most famous for his books *Dr. Jekyll and Mr. Hyde* and *Treasure Island*, describes a voyage of discovery he took as a young man through the Cévennes mountain range in France. About the purpose of his journey, he writes:

> *For my part, I travel not to go anywhere, but to go. I travel for travel's sake. The great affair is to move; to feel the needs and hitches of our life more nearly; to come down off this feather-bed of civilisation, and find the globe granite underfoot and strewn with cutting flints.*

Jack Kerouac employs roads and transport as central themes in several of his novels, which are in many ways also journeys. In *The Dharma Bums*, for example, he uses the expression, "the meditation of the trail." The path is a symbol of freedom and adventure; it's the opposite of standstill and conformity. It's not strange that Kerouac became an icon for young Americans wishing to break with their parents' generation, which told them security, predictability, settling down, and the accumulation of capital were the primary tasks of life.

I CHECKED THE map and saw that I had reached the halfway point of my long walk. I still had quite a stretch ahead of me before I would reach the cabin, but I was in no hurry, I had more than enough time.

Here I was, walking along the path in search of the forest's peace. I was a wandering cliché, as if I had been copied and pasted from a 1950s folk song. I whistled and talked out loud to myself. In doing so, I broke one of my own rules about not talking out loud to myself when walking on paths; however, because this path was particularly long, I granted myself an exception. Figuratively speaking, I had a piece of straw in the corner of my mouth, a tattered hat on my head, and a sack slung over my shoulder. I chatted my way through my own life, discussing to myself my work, family, friends, and finances. What areas of my life could I improve? How could I improve as a person? Father? Partner? Friend? I arrived at a conclusion that from now on I should set the following goals in life: To become a vegetarian. Be debt-free by fifty. Never be short-tempered and angry with my children. Hardly ever be short-tempered and angry with my partner. Visit my father more often. Never kill animals. Wear shoes as infrequently as possible. My walking and the path made everything simpler. I was in the flow, and I enjoyed every step.

The path is the goal, and the goal is the path. I was so high-spirited that I turned into a wandering producer of new path metaphors. I started thinking about a song my mother always sang for my sisters and me, sometimes when we were walking but most often when we were driving in the car, bored out of our minds in the back seat. I liked the romantic nature of the song; it made it seem as though life was simple and carefree. I wanted to be the narrator of the song. I envied him his worry-free attitude, and as I ambled along the trail, I realized this was the closest I had ever come to that state. The words to the song go something like this:

> I am the happy wanderer, as free from cares I go,
> along the endless country path, I like to walk so slow.
> . . .
> I am the happy wanderer, O, heaven be content
> to let me walk along this path until the very end.

Romanticism's idealization of the wanderer, the vagabond, the wayfarer was also about the importance of getting closer to humankind's original purpose.

The Romantics felt an undefined sense that we were born to walk, to wander through life, to meet new people, to see new landscape—a feeling the English environmentalist and author George Monbiot refers to as a "genetic memory." The arena was nature and the activity was walking and, seen from this perspective, one can say that the Romantic wanderers protesting against societal conformity abandoned the habit of settling down and instead reclaimed their ancestors' nomadic existence, perhaps without even realizing it.

Romanticism has been forced to endure a lot of criticism for its overemphasis on nature as an inspiration and redeemer of grand emotions expressed through art. While some of this criticism is undoubtedly deserved, some of it is unreasonable because it fails to take into account the period during which Romanticism developed. Every new cultural current arises as a reaction to something else, a break with the status quo, and this is the same for Romanticism. It came about at a time when European spiritual and social life was characterized by an almost unprecedented philosophy of advancement and unrestrained exploitation of natural resources. Romanticism was a protest against industrialization and mechanization, road construction and expansion; it was a voice for the path at a time when roads threatened to take over. The protest was expressed through the works of poets who are still regarded as the most significant in European literary history: William Wordsworth. Jean-Jacques Rousseau. Friedrich Hölderlin. Johann Wolfgang von Goethe.

On September 6, 1780, Goethe notched a little poem into the log wall of a hunting lodge on Kickelhahn mountain in Germany. I have had a special relationship to this poem, "Wanderer's Nightsong," ever since my German uncle read it aloud for me one summer's day many years ago, at the farm near the lake at the little cabin where I was now headed. This version has been translated into English by Henry Wadsworth Longfellow:

> *O'er all the hill-tops*
> *Is quiet now,*
> *In all the tree-tops*
> *Hearest thou*
> *Hardly a breath;*
> *The birds are asleep in the trees:*
> *Wait; soon like these*
> *Thou too shalt rest.*

✦

FOURTEEN HOURS HAD passed since I left the hotel that morning in Larvik. My feet moved, time passed, the sun went down behind the mountains in the west.

I began to feel the exhaustion. It was not the type of exhaustion that comes from running. There was no lactic acid, no stiff muscles, no oxygen deficiency, only a mild sleepiness, a cozy feeling that the stores of energy in my body were beginning to empty.

I walked down to the lake and sat on a hill with a view out to the west. Far away, on the opposite shore, I could see the island where John and I had spent the night on our hazardous canoe trip thirty years ago.

I stood and continued. Eventually I found myself inside a dense deciduous forest. Where there had once been a path it was now overgrown, but I remembered the way and soon the forest opened up and I emerged onto a field. Now I knew just where I was. I recognized this place.

The first flowers of spring lined the edge of the forest, and on the opposite side of the field was the house where my grandmother was born. That was in 1925, between the First and Second World Wars. She was brought up there with her family, only a few miles east of the farm where my grandfather grew up. There weren't many people who lived in these parts back then. Grandma and Grandpa could not have avoided meeting as children and teenagers. They began courting, they got married, my mother was born, and the fact that these small events took place were the reason that I was here now, whistling and walking through the forest on this mild spring evening.

A gravel road ran along the downward slope of the field. This had once been a path and a wagon track, but that was before my time. I only ever knew it as a gravel road, and I find it strange but wonderful that it's never been paved.

I followed the gravel road down, and soon I could see the north end of the lake through the trees. It was getting dark out. A blackbird sang from the treetops. The grass was cold and wet. I veered to the right, walked along a field, under the trees, and there, in the dim twilight of the spring evening, in a clearing with a view toward the lake, stood the little cabin from my childhood, silent and abandoned beneath the dark trees.

THE CABIN WAS just as I'd remembered it. The smell, the light; nothing had changed. Living room, kitchen, bedroom, hallway. A handwoven rug hung on the living room wall in shades of brown and red and green, in a pattern I had never understood. An old woodstove sat in the kitchen, cast iron, faded and dried out, almost gray against the white chimney wall. The elk antlers were above the fireplace, brown and white and rough, four prongs. Once it had been the largest set of antlers I'd ever seen. And there stood the wall lamp that my father had made from a gnarled old root he had found on the path.

I finished off the rest of my food, took off my dirty clothes, and lay down on the sofa in the living room. Before I fell asleep, I thought about the old photograph I had seen at my father's kitchen table one year earlier.

IT IS EASTER. The year is 1977. I have just turned six; my sisters are five and four. We are sitting on the sofa in the cabin because my father wants to take a picture. He has positioned us close together, the way he always did when he wanted to take a picture, at all of our birthday parties, every Christmas Eve, on every holiday and celebration. He took hundreds of photos like this one; he could never get enough of them.

My sisters and I are sitting on the sofa, and on the coffee table in front of us is the cage with the parakeet Jakob. Jakob was a pretty bird, blue and white, the only pet I've ever owned. Two years after the picture was taken, he came down with a mysterious optical illness that made him go blind. He sat perched on his peg wondering what had happened, why everything was suddenly so dark, and one evening during our summer vacation a few years later, my father twisted his neck to free him from his suffering.

It wasn't until the next day that I discovered the empty cage.

"Where is Jakob?" I asked. "Where is Jakob?"

My mother was the one to tell me what had happened. She explained that Jakob had been suffering as a blind bird. That sometimes freeing a creature from its suffering is the right thing to do. "It's better for Jakob to die than to keep living," said my mother. She was wearing a gray-and-white-striped cardigan and we sat together on the steps of the cabin and it was dusk. My mother's face was serious, but mild. "That's life," she said, and for the first time I understood that death exists, and that it would one day come for us all. Big and small alike. Parakeets and people.

I buried Jakob in the field behind the cabin where the path starts. A little wooden cross under the pine trees was all that was left of him. From that day on, they became one and the same, Jakob and the path, linked together in my young mind. The path reminded me of Jakob. Jakob reminded me of the path. I couldn't think of one without thinking about the other.

In the old picture my father took, I am as yet happily ignorant of the fate of the parakeet. Jakob is perched on the peg in his cage. My sisters and I are on the sofa. We stare into the camera. My sisters have their pale, almost white hair in pigtails. My bangs are uneven, and I am wearing a wool sweater that is too short in the arms.

The camera says click, the flash lights up the room, and my father smiles contentedly.

My mother is in the kitchen. We cannot see her from where we are sitting, but we know that she and my father have talked about what is going to happen next.

"Get dressed, we are going for a walk," calls my mother.

We protest, my sisters and I. It's so comfortable there on the sofa, the fireplace is warm, and there's music on the radio. We are enjoying our sedentary state. Why should we go outside now?

"Come on," says my father, "get off the sofa. A little bit of movement is good for everyone."

+

I AWOKE BECAUSE of the sharp sunlight on my face. I stood up from the sofa but had to sit down again. My leg muscles were sore from the previous day's endless walk; it felt like someone had stuck a knife into each leg and it was impossible to stand up.

I stretched on the sofa, trying to get some life back into my muscles and warm and loosen them up. The spring sunshine slanted through the living room

windows. Dust danced in the dry air and from somewhere flies were buzzing.

I put on my socks and tried standing again. This
time it went better. I staggered slowly into the kitchen
with stiff leg joints, the way small children do when
they have to go to the bathroom really badly. My body
felt heavy; the floor was like ice. While the water boiled,
I walked slowly back and forth between the rooms. I
lifted objects, opened cupboards, ran my hand over
the old wood paneling. Some things had changed, but
I could remember everything as it used to be. Pots,
cups, old tablecloths. The wallpaper in the kitchen: yellow buttercups against a pale background. The 1950s
cooking range, and on top of the old woodstove an
enormous kettle, the kind that was used to boil coffee
for large functions. Inside the fuse box, there were only
four fuses. Inside the cupboard in the hallway were
mosquito coils from another time.

From the bedroom window I could see where the
path begins. The window was covered with mosquito
netting when I was a child. The mosquito netting was
gone now, but I remember that it was made out of a stiff
green material, and that my mother had once repaired
it. A seam ran along the lower right corner. It curved
across the netting like a path on a map.

YOU CAN'T
WALK THE SAME
PATH TWICE

POURED COFFEE INTO a mug and went back into the living room. On top of the coffee table was the cabin book, green and faded. The gray penciled handwriting was almost illegible. The book is as old as I am. It contains the history of my family, detailed descriptions from our vacations and weekends, what we did and who was visiting, some episodes that I can still remember and some I have long since forgotten. Stories about the path, year after year.

I sat down and leafed through the cabin book. Its spine was fraying. Yellowing pages stuck out. On a white area on the cover, my mother had written the name of our cabin, *Solli.*

I let the pages flutter through my fingers. My father's even, straight handwriting. My mother's, soft, curvy. My sisters' drawings of girls with big eyes and red lips. My own drawings of paths and land-scapes, always peopleless, rendered in green, brown, black, and blue: a young boy's dream of a perfect world.

THE CABIN WAS built in 1952. My grandfather bought it in May 1971 and gave it to his children. It has been in my family for as long as I have been alive, and the same cabin book is still in use. It's almost completely full now; there are only a few pages left.

I found my name on the very first page of the book. I was three months old when my mother wrote the first entry.

June 24, 1971. Inger-Lene, Åge, and Torbjørn spent the night here for the first time.

And then, the following year:

April 29, 1972. We went for a little walk on the path with Torbjørn in the backpack carrier. Torbjørn likes to toddle around, eating leaves and moss, and pine-cones, which are apparently the best.

I continued to leaf through the pages. The book was the history of our lives. Everything was written down here. My sisters were born; we became a family of four, and then five. We visited the cabin in the spring, summer, fall, and winter. The entries were almost all the same. We entertained guests. We had a barbecue. We went boating. We made a bonfire. We picked mushrooms. We picked berries. We went fishing. There was sunshine or rain, lots of mosquitos or very few, the well was always dry, everything is always wonderful, we always take a little walk on the path.

The years go by.

April 4–11, Easter 1977. Inger-Lene, Åge, Torbjørn, Vigdis, Anne, and Jakob the parakeet have spent Easter up here. The weather was cold the whole time, just above freezing every morning. Sunshine every day but with a cold northern wind. Nonetheless, we have had a lovely time, adults and children alike.

May 22. We picked the first lilies of the year.

August 5–7. Went blueberry picking. It will be nice to have the blueberries throughout the winter.

August 29–31. The five of us have enjoyed another weekend at the cabin. We passed time collecting cranberries and mushrooms.

And then, during the summer holiday of 1979:

Something sad happened during our vacation too. Jakob is dead. He was sick, so it was better for him to die.

"You cannot step into the same river twice" is among the most well-known phrases in Western philosophy. It was the Greek philosopher Heraclitus who first expressed this, or wrote it down, 500 years BC. Heraclitus meant that the world's and nature's innermost nature is change, and that change arises through opposites: day and night, wet and dry, warm and cold, summer and winter. Opposites are mutually dependent. Something that is low exists only in relation to something that is higher. Something is dark only because something else is lighter.

You cannot step into the same river twice.

I never understood what Heraclitus meant with his famous phrase, so whenever anyone mentions it I have always nodded and tried to change the subject as quickly as possible. The fact that the river is always new because new water is constantly flowing through it seems fairly obvious, so just how clever could this saying be?

Heraclitus was cleverer than that, and as I sat near the starting point of the path, the phrase finally took on new meaning for me. It isn't the river that changes; it is the one who steps into it. Heraclitus is talking about people, not about rivers and water. We cannot visit the same place twice because the place is colored by who we are when we come to it, and we are always someone else, never the same. "You cannot step into the same river twice" could also have been "You cannot walk the same path twice."

+

MY MOTHER DIED in the winter of 2010. She was buried on a Thursday at the beginning of March. It had been a cold winter. Flecks of snow covered the churchyard, but spring was in the air and a chickadee sang from a naked birch tree above our heads. We stood on the yellow grass of the previous summer while the priest said a few words about life and death that I no longer remember, before my mother's coffin was lowered into the earth.

I leafed through the cabin book and came to her final entry. Springtime the year before she died. She didn't know it would be her last visit. My sisters and I had long since grown up and now it was only my mother and father who frequented the little cabin.

May 10, 2009. Åge and Inger-Lene came for a brief day trip. A gorgeous spring day with green leaves, wood anemones, lilies of the valley, and birdsong.

I put down the cabin book and went into the bedroom. There was only a single bed. It was a bunkbed; it was where my sisters and I slept. The two of them shared the bottom bunk and I was on top. My father slept on the sofa in the living room, and my mother slept on a mattress in a doorway, with her head in the bedroom and her feet in the kitchen.

I went back into the living room and sat down on the sofa. I continued reading the book. My father had written an entry only a few weeks after my mother's death. He did what people always do whenever sorrow is too hard to bear. He had to get out, had to walk, had to go visit places that had been of significance in his and my mother's lives. The cabin held their history, and so this was naturally where he would come in hopes that this place might bring him closer to her.

I think he was like me. I can hardly think about the path without thinking of my mother. She made the path the centerpiece of a land full of adventure. How many times have I walked on the path? I can't put a number on it. I only know that those family walks have been the highlights of my life.

April 10–11, 2010. Åge spent the night here for the first time this year. It is strange to be here alone, but Solli is a place I have always loved to visit, and I have so many good memories from this place. Thank you, I'll be back soon.

✦

WE THINK OF a path as the way to something else, toward the future and whatever lies ahead. But a path also points backward, to the time and the place we came from. When we walk on it, we are taking part in a universal and timeless act. We walk through the landscape that has formed us and the people who have formed us and those who came before us, through work and leisure time, curiosity, and escape.

There's a story in Greek mythology about Theseus and Ariadne. Ariadne was the daughter of King
Minos of Crete. She fell in love with the hero Theseus
when he came to Crete to fight the Minotaur, a dread-
ful half-human, half-ox creature that King Minos had
locked inside a labyrinth from which it was impossible
to escape. Ariadne knew this. She gave Theseus the end
of a ball of string to take with him as he entered the
labyrinth. As he walked, he unraveled the yarn behind
him along the route. After killing the Minotaur, Theseus turned and followed the yarn back out. The yarn
was a path. It helped him to find his way.

*And in this way, with the virgin Ariadne's help, the
entrance that no other adventurer had ever again
found was reached by rolling up the thread...*

I pulled down the blinds in the living room and left
the cabin book on the table. I put my coffee cup on the
counter. It was a ritual my mother and father always
used to have. Everything had to be tidied up before
we left to go back home after a weekend or vacation.
Once that was done, once everything was washed and
tidied and we were ready to go, they would make one
last cup of coffee and they would leave those two cups,
unwashed, until the next time we came.

I put the coffee cup down on the counter the way they used to do. I pulled on my boots in the entryway. Then I went outside, shouldered my backpack, turned toward the path, and began to walk.

DISCOVERY
AT THE
JOURNEY'S END

———

THE PATH AS I remembered it was gone. It had vanished; maybe it had never existed at all. The parakeet Jakob had long since turned to dust. There was no trace of the first bridge that crossed the creek. There was no trace of the second bridge. Even the creek seemed strange. It no longer babbled softly beneath the uppermost bridge, and there weren't any cowslips along its banks. The waterfall was gone. Although the creek brimmed with snowmelt from the spring, there was no waterfall to be seen, only tiny rapids, and the creek was no more than a foot and a half wide. It flowed toward the bottom of the valley, but it didn't froth the way I remembered it.

The field no longer existed. The place that marked the end of the path, where we would pause and eat our packed lunches and chocolate, was now overgrown. We used to be able to sense the echoes of people who had once worked the earth here. Whose backs had bent under the sun, cutting the grass with their scythes and hanging it to dry on racks, eating their lunches in a shady spot, sweating and enduring, enjoying coffee breaks and quiet conversations, listening to the birds singing in the forest and the insects' eternal buzzing, the horse that shifted nervously and the dog that dashed happily around.

I stood under the pine trees where the field had once been. The trees were silent and as tall as apartment buildings. They grew clustered together, and beneath them the ground was empty and still. Grass, flowers, straw, and deciduous trees were all gone. The path as I remembered it had vanished. The only place where it still remained was in my memory and those of a few other people.

I turned around and walked back to the cabin. I crossed the creek twice and when I came to the mountain where the horse used to rest, I stopped. The mountain was the way I remembered it. Four decades is no time at all for a mountain that has stood unchanged since the ice melted and the land rose up. I walked over to the mountain. I ran my hand along the cold stone surface and leaned my back up against the mountain wall. There was no cooling breeze, even now.

✦

BACK IN THE office a few days later, I went to the Norwegian Trekking Association website. One of its many features is that it allows you to measure the distance between two points on a map.

I looked up the location of the cabin. The cabin was marked as a black dot on the green map. The creek was a thin blue line, but I didn't see any path. I put the arrow on top of the cabin and dragged it to the spot where the little field had once been, the spot that marked the end of the path. The distance that came up surprised me: 1,154 feet in a straight line. A mere 1,154 feet. Measured against the actual terrain, the path was maybe only a quarter of a mile long.

I measured the distance one more time. It was and is 1,154 feet, and while I sat in the office staring at my computer screen, I realized I had just stumbled onto a truth I had never before understood. I had come to the end of the journey. Only then did it become clear to me that the history of the path is longer than the path itself.

ON WRITING
THIS BOOK

———————

A BOOK ABOUT paths cannot be written entirely from a desk. On the other hand, writing does require sitting down, at least occasionally. This book has been at the intersection of these two very different states. I wrote it on a computer while sitting in a chair at a desk, but the ideas, thoughts, reflections, and associations came to me while walking.

The French philosopher Jean-Jacques Rousseau claimed he could only think when walking. The English scientist Charles Darwin spoke about "the thinking path," and thereby joined the two states of thinking and walking. And while I don't mean to put myself in league with either Rousseau or Darwin, I am also someone whose head works best when I am on foot.

I have walked on paths through the forest and on sidewalks in the city. Every time a new thought arises, I have stopped to write it down before continuing on, because if there's one thing I've learned, it's this: if you don't immediately take note of such thoughts, they will slip away into the great void and be gone forever. Thoughts don't arise from sitting on a sofa. Thoughts arise when you walk, as if there is some mysterious link between these two fundamental human activities, walking and thinking. Because of this, among other things, it is slightly disturbing that people in our day and age primarily tend to sit still.

GRATITUDE

I HAVE MANY people to thank for the existence of this book, but if it contains any factual errors, I have only myself to blame.

Thank you to Kenneth Buch, the coach of the Norwegian National Orienteering Team, who told me about what it means to read the landscape and the mental challenges that go along with finding one's way through terrain without paths. To Dag O. Hessen, professor at the Institute for Biology at the University of Oslo, who educated me about movement and migration. Bjørn Amsrud, the first person to walk the length of Norway and from whom I had the pleasure of hearing about his long journey. Anette L'Orsa, who told me about her long hike on the Pacific Crest Trail. Thank you to Carine Eymundsson, at the Institute for Archeology at the University of Oslo, who showed me around the Historic Museum and spoke about the first people who came to Norway following the last Ice Age. Thanks to Per Bremnes, hobby historian and expert on the ancient Nordmannsslepene traffic routes across the Hardanger Plateau. Thank you to Vibeke Fürst Haugen and Agnete Brun, who related their five-week-long pilgrimage along the Camino de Santiago. To Anne Marie van Baal and Svein Lysebo, who helped me with valuable information about my grandparents' farm. Tarje Holtvedt and Kjetil Østli, who read the manuscript and offered me invaluable feedback along the way. Thank you to my editor, Mari Bjørkeng, who took care to keep me on track when I almost lost sight of it while writing. Thank you to my hiking buddy and pathfinder, John Kenneth Stigum. Thank you to Vigdis and Anne for good memories. Thank you to Mamma and Pappa, who brought me along on the path and taught me to walk.

NOTES

I FIRST LEARNED the history of the tracks at Mistaken Point, which I describe on page 1, from Robert Moor's book *On Trails: An Exploration.* I have also taken information from James O'Donoghue's article "Found: The first ever animal trails," published in *New Scientist,* February 4, 2010. I first set eyes on the tracks I describe in a photograph owned by Oxford University. For those interested, it may be viewed here: https://www.newscientist.com/article/dn18479-found-the-first-ever-animal-trails/.

The Peter Wessel Zapffe quotation on page 6 is from "Veien" ("The Road") published in *Barske glæder.* Excerpt from *Barske Glæder Og andre temaer fra et liv under åpen himmel* (*Rough Joys and other themes from a life lived under an open sky*) by Peter Wessel Zapffe © Oslo, 1969, English translation by Becky L. Crook © 2020. Originally published by Gyldendal. Used by permission of Cappelen Damm.

Some readers may recognize the formulation "the great, godless land" on page 23. I took this from Knut Hamsun's Nobel Prize–winning novel *Growth of the Soil*.

Quotes from Agnete Brun and Vibeke Fürst Haugen on page 33 were shared with the author. English translation by Becky L. Crook © 2020. Used by permission of Agnete Brun and Vibeke Fürst Haugen.

Information on page 35 about the distances of the Norwegian Trekking Association trail network is from the Norwegian Trekking Association.

I got the information on page 36 about the total distance of Norwegian trails from the Norwegian Public Roads Administration (Statens Vegvesen).

Excerpts on pages 40–41 and 162 from *Stier, mennesker og naturopplevelser* by Annette Bischoff, © Annette Bischoff 2015. English translation by Becky L. Crook © 2020. Used by permission of Annette Bischoff.

Quotes from Anette L'Orsa on page 43 were shared with the author. English translation by Becky L. Crook © 2020. Used by permission of Anette L'Orsa.

Excerpts on page 93 from Robert Frost's poem were taken from www.poetryfoundation.org. The perspective on page 94 about the broad popular misunderstanding of "The Road Not Taken" is general knowledge among those interested in poetry. I have primarily used the arguments from Robert Faggen's analysis, to which I refer in the text, and from the little pamphlet entitled *Wellspring: Poetry for the Journey* authored by Allison Seay, Associate for Religion and the Arts, St. Stephen's Episcopal

Church, 2016. Faggen's analysis of "The Road Not Taken" was published at Modern American Poetry, www.modernamerican-poetry.org.

Excerpt on page 140 from *Sporten* by Rune Slagstad, © Rune Slagstad 2008. English translation by Becky L. Crook © 2020. Used by permission of Pax Forlag.

The excerpt from "Jotunheimen" by Emanuel Mohr on page 140 appeared in *Den Norske Turistforenings Årbok 1944*, a travel magazine put out by the Norwegian Travel Association. English translation by Becky L. Crook. Used by permission of Den Norske Turistforening.

The Norwegian podcast "Two White Men," to which I refer on page 143, is produced by the Norwegian channel NRK.

The details on pages 145 to 148 about Emma Gatewood, the first woman to walk the Appalachian Trail, were taken from Ben Montgomery's biography, *Grandma Gatewood's Walk: The Inspiring Story of the Woman Who Saved the Appalachian Trail*, Chicago Review Press, 2014, as well as from Diana Reese's article, "Grandma Gatewood Survived Domestic Violence To Walk the Appalachian Trail Alone at 67," published in the *Washington Post* in January 2015.

Quotes from Bjørn Amsrud on pages 150 and 151, as recorded by the author. English translation by Becky L. Crook © 2020. Used by permission of Bjørn Amsrud.

The facts and quotes about my grandparents' farm on page 155 were taken from *Hedrum Bygdebok 3. Gårder og slekter i Kvelde og Hvarnes sogn*, 1979, digital version from the Norwegian National Library.

The Shakespeare quote on page 161 was taken from *As You Like It*, Act II, Scene VII.

The quote attributed to Arne Næss on page 161 is paraphrased from *Life's Philosophy: Reason and Feeling in a Deeper World.*

"The Happy Wanderer" song I refer to on page 197 was originally a German song called "Der fröliche Wanderer," or "Mein Vater ist ein Wandersmann." The song was written by Friedrich Sigismund at the start of the 1800s and put to music by Friedrich-Wilhelm Möller just after the Second World War. The Norwegian text, which was sung by my mother, was written by Jacob Helte. The English translation here was done by Becky L. Crook, though the song does not exist in English.

The Johann Wolfgang von Goethe poem that I quote on page 199 is one of two poems with the title "Wanderer's Nightsong," both written in 1776. The Norwegian version with which I was familiar was translated into Norwegian by the famous writer André Bjerke. This English translation was done by Henry Wadsworth Longfellow and was taken from Bartleby.com.

The sentence on page 212: "I can hardly think about the path without thinking of my mother. She made the path the centerpiece of a land full of adventure" is a rewrite of two sentences taken from the story "The Mountain Lake" in Johannes Dahl's book *Nordmarka. Eventyr og Eldorado*, Johan Grundt Tanum, 1942.

On page 213, a few small facts that I had forgotten about the myth of Ariadne and Theseus were taken from snl.no and Wikipedia. The Roman poet Ovid is one of many who have interpreted this myth. The quote on page 213 was taken from an English translation of his writing found on the internet (trans. Miller; book VIII, lines 172–76).

Where no other sources are given, English translations have been done by Becky L. Crook, the English translator of this book.

The photograph of my sisters and me on the path was, as the very attentive reader may already have realized, taken by my father.

SOURCES

Bischoff, Annette. *Stier, mennesker og naturopplevelser*. Novus Forlag, 2015.

Bjerknes, Ernst. *Via Skis, Velocipede and Sketchbook*. Dybwad, 1943.

Bryson, Bill. *A Walk in the Woods: Rediscovering America on the Appalachian Trail*. Black Swan, 2015.

Chamberlin, Silas. *On the Trail: A History of American Hiking*. Yale University Press, 2016.

Chatwin, Bruce. *The Songlines*. Vintage Books, 1998.

Dingle, Hugh. *Migration: The Biology of Life on the Move*. Oxford University Press, 2014.

Emerson, Ralph Waldo, and Henry David Thoreau. *Nature* and *Walking*. Beacon Press, 1992.

Fønnebø, Reidar. *Langs Nordmannsslepene over Hardangervidda*. Universitetsforlaget, 1988. (Excerpt translated here and in other places by B. L. Crook.)

Fønnebø, Reidar. *Nordmannsslepene. Store Nordmanns Slepa, den eldgamle ferdselsåren mellom Østlandet og Vestlandet.* Norges Naturvernforbund og Numedal Reiselivslag, 1968.

Foy, George Michelsen. *Finding North: How Navigation Makes Us Human.* Flatiron Books, 2016.

Gatty, Harold. *Finding Your Way Without Map or Compass.* Dover Publications, 1983.

Gooley, Tristan. *How to Read Nature: Awaken Your Senses to the Outdoors You've Never Noticed.* The Experiment. New York, 2017.

Hamsun, Knut. *Growth of the Soil.* Penguin Classics, 2007.

Harari, Yuval Noah. *Sapiens: A Brief History of Humankind.* Signal 2014.

Harris, Nick, Helen Harris, and Paul Marshall. *A Man in a Hurry: The Extraordinary Life and Times of Edward Payson Weston, the World's Greatest Walker.* deCoubertin Books, 2012.

Heinrich, Bernd. *The Homing Instinct: Meaning and Mystery in Animal Migration.* Mariner Books, 2015.

Kerouac, Jack. *The Dharma Bums.* Penguin Classics, 1976.

Koester, Robert J. *Lost Person Behavior: A Search and Rescue Guide on Where to Look—For Land, Air and Water.* dbS Productions, Charlottesville, Virginia, 2008.

Macfarlane, Robert. *The Old Ways: A Journey on Foot.* Penguin Books, 2012.

Monbiot, George. *Feral: Rewilding the Land, Sea, and Human Life.* Penguin Books, 2013.

Montgomery, Ben. *Grandma Gatewood's Walk: The Inspiring Story of the Woman Who Saved the Appalachian Trail.* Chicago Review Press, 2014.

Moor, Robert. *On Trails: An Exploration.* New York: Simon & Schuster, 2016.

Næss, Arne. *Life's Philosophy: Reason and Feeling in a Deeper World.* University of Georgia Press, 2008.

Nicholson, Geoff. *The Lost Art of Walking: The History, Science, Philosophy, Literature, Theory and Practice of Pedestrianism.* Harbour Books, 2011.

Øverås, Tor Eystein. *I dette landskap. Artikler og essays.* Gyldendal, 2012.

Solnit, Rebecca. *A Field Guide to Getting Lost.* Penguin Books, 2006.

Solnit, Rebecca. *Wanderlust: A History of Walking.* Penguin Books, 2000.

Stevenson, J. R. *Travels with a Donkey in the Cévennes.* Penguin Books, 1976.

Thoreau, Henry David. *Walden; Or, Life in the Woods.* Signet Classic, 1980.